# The
# Respiratory
# System

# The
# Respiratory
# System

# Titles in the Understanding the Human Body series include:

Understanding
**THE HUMAN BODY**

# The
# Respiratory
# System

Pam Walker and Elaine Wood

**LUCENT
BOOKS ®**

**THOMSON**
━━━━ ✳ ━━━━ ™
**GALE**

San Diego • Detroit • New York • San Francisco • Cleveland • New Haven, Conn. • Waterville, Maine • London • Munich

On cover: A powerful swimmer puts his respiratory system to the test.

**LIBRARY OF CONGRESS CATALOGING-IN-PUBLICATION DATA**

Walker, Pam, 1958–
    The respiratory system / by Pam Walker and Elaine Wood.
       p. cm. — (Understanding the human body)
Includes bibliographical references and index.
Summary: Discusses the organs and function of the human respiratory system, respiratory events such as sneezes and yawns, breathing under extreme conditions,
and medical treatments of respiratory disorders.
    ISBN 1-59018-153-0
1. Respiratory organs—Juvenile literature. [1. Respiratory organs. 2. Respiration.]
I. Wood, Elaine, 1950– II. Title. III. Series.
    QP121 .W34 2003
    612.2—dc21

2001007311

Printed in the United States of America

# CONTENTS

# FOREWORD

Since Earth first formed, countless creatures have come and gone. Dinosaurs and other types of land and sea animals all fell prey to climatic shifts, food shortages, and myriad other environmental factors. However, one species—human beings—survived throughout tens of thousands of years of evolution, adjusting to changes in climate and moving when food was scarce. The primary reason human beings were able to do this is that they possess a complex and adaptable brain and body.

The human body is comprised of organs, tissue, and bone that work independently and together to sustain life. Although it is both remarkable and unique, the human body shares features with other living organisms: the need to eat, breathe, and eliminate waste; the need to reproduce and eventually die.

Human beings, however, have many characteristics that other living creatures do not. The adaptable brain is responsible for these characteristics. Human beings, for example, have excellent memories; they can recall events that took place twenty, thirty, even fifty years earlier. Human beings also possess a high level of intelligence. Their unique capacity to invent, create, and innovate has led to discoveries and inventions such as vaccines, automobiles, and computers. And the human brain allows people to feel and respond to a variety of emotions. No other creature on Earth has such a broad range of abilities.

Although the human brain physically resembles a large, soft walnut, its capabilities seem limitless. The brain controls the body's movement, enabling humans to sprint, jog, walk, and crawl. It controls the body's internal functions, allowing people to breathe and maintain a heartbeat without effort. And it controls a person's creative talent, giving him or her the ability to write novels, paint masterpieces, or compose music.

Like a computer, the brain runs a network of body systems that keep human beings alive. The nervous system relays the brain's messages to the rest of the body. The respiratory system draws in life-sustaining oxygen and expels carbon dioxide waste. The circulatory system carries that oxygen to and from the body's vital organs. The reproductive system allows humans to continue their species and flourish as the dominant creatures on the planet. The digestive system takes in vital nutrients and converts them into the energy the body needs to grow. And the immune system protects the body from disease and foreign objects. When all of these systems work properly, the result is an intricate, extraordinary living machine.

Even when some of the systems are not working properly, the human body can often adapt. Healthy people have two kidneys, but, if necessary, they can live with just one. Doctors can remove a defective liver, heart, lung, or pancreas and replace it with a working one from another body. And a person blinded by an accident, disease, or birth defect can live a perfectly normal life by developing other senses to make up for the loss of sight.

The human body adapts to countless external factors as well. It sweats to cool off, adjusts the level of oxygen it needs at high altitudes, and derives nutritional value from a wide variety of foods, making do with what is available in a given region.

Only under tremendous duress does the human body cease to function. Extreme fluctuations in temperature, an invasion by hardy germs, or severe physical damage can halt normal bodily functions and cause death. Yet, even in such circumstances, the body continues to try to repair itself. The body of a diabetic, for example, will take in extra liquid and try to expel excess glucose through the urine. And a body exposed to extremely low temperatures will shiver in an effort to generate its own heat.

Lucent's Understanding the Human Body series explores different systems of the human body. Each volume describes the parts of a given body system and how they work both individually and collectively. Unique characteristics, malfunctions, and cutting edge medical procedures and technologies are also discussed. Photographs, diagrams, and glossaries enhance the text, and annotated bibliographies provide readers with opportunities for further discussion and research.

# Journey Through the Human Respiratory System

Without oxygen in the air, a great number of the familiar life forms on earth would not exist. Plants and animals, as well as thousands of other living things, require oxygen. Paramecia and other simple one-celled organisms absorb oxygen directly from the atmosphere. The oxygen passes through the cell membrane into the cell, where it is used to help convert food to energy. The cycle of taking in oxygen and putting it to use, called oxygen metabolism, results in two waste products, carbon dioxide and water. Simple organisms expel the wastes directly into their surroundings through the cell membranes.

Like paramecia and other one-celled organisms, human cells also require oxygen and produce wastes. Yet most of a human's cells are too far from the body's surface to absorb oxygen directly from the environment or to release carbon dioxide and water directly into it. Therefore humans and other multi-celled organisms have developed a sophisticated process for accomplishing these tasks. This process is called respiration. The lungs and other body part that make respiration possible are known as the respiratory system.

## The Breath of Life

The terms "respiration" and "breathing" are sometimes used interchangeably, but they actually have different meanings. Breathing, only one part of respiration, describes the process by which air enters and leaves the lungs. Respiration refers to the entire procedure of acquiring oxygen, delivering it to cells, using it within the cells to make energy, and disposing of the resulting waste products.

The gas exchange between the human body and the environment takes place in the respiratory system, where life-sustaining oxygen is taken from the air and delivered to cells in the bloodstream. And it is where carbon dioxide and water, the normal waste products of oxygen metabolism, are taken from cells in the bloodstream and released into the environment. The respiratory system is like a factory that works twenty-four hours a day, seven days a week, to keep the body supplied with oxygen. There is no room for malfunction in this factory. If the body is deprived of air for more than three or four minutes, the brain and other organs are damaged. After five minutes, death can result.

Respiration occurs in several stages. In the first step, air is brought into the body through the upper respiratory tract. This section of the respiratory system includes the nose, mouth, throat, and windpipe, or trachea.

## The Upper Respiratory Tract

For respiration to occur, oxygen from the air must get into the body. The air we breathe is a little over 75 percent nitrogen. Carbon dioxide and other gases comprise 1 percent. The remainder is oxygen. All the gases in the air except oxygen enter and leave the body unchanged. Only oxygen is captured by the body and used in respiration.

The upper respiratory system serves as a passage for air traveling to and from the lungs. The respiratory tract begins at the nose and mouth. Air entering through the nose passes over specialized cells of the nasal mucosa. These cells filter and moisten air, then warm it to body temperature. The nose is divided into two cavities by tissue called the nasal septum. The roof of each nasal cavity contains olfactory nerves that are responsible for the sense of smell. They carry impulses from the nose to the brain, which interprets the odors. Nasal cavities also connect to the sinus cavities. These are air-containing spaces in the skull. Like the nose, each sinus cavity is lined with nasal mucosa.

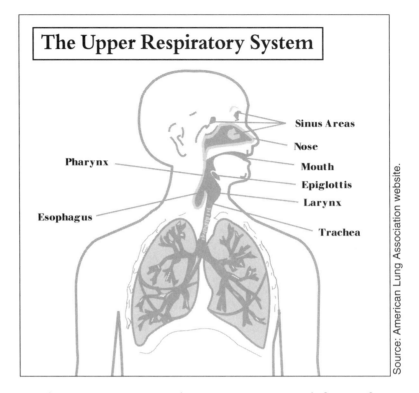

**The Upper Respiratory System**

Sinus Areas

Nose

Pharynx

Mouth

Epiglottis

Larynx

Esophagus

Trachea

Source: American Lung Association website.

The respiratory system has some impressive defensive features for removing foreign matter. Hairs in the nose trap large particles of dirt. Mucosa or mucous membranes lining the nose, sinuses, pharynx, larynx, and trachea help keep the airways clean in two ways. They contain goblet cells, which secrete a thick substance called mucus that traps dust particles. More than twenty-five teaspoons of mucus are made every day. As an additional deterrent to invading particles, hairlike projections called cilia extend from the outermost layers of mucous membrane cells. Cilia work relentlessly, brushing debris that enters the respiratory system back toward the mouth and nose at a rate of one to two centimeters each minute.

## Air's Passageways

The nose and throat open into a combined area called the pharynx. This is a muscular passageway for both the respiratory and digestive systems. At the lower end of the pharynx are two openings: one for air and one for food. It is important that air and food travel through the correct tubes. An opening at the base of the pharynx is called the glottis. When food is swallowed, a small flap of cartilage, the epiglottis, covers the glottis to keep food out of the lungs. Air travels through the glottis to the larynx.

The larynx, or voice box, plays an important role in the respiratory process. It provides a second gate of protection to keep food and liquid out of the airway. Structurally, it contains two sets of folded tissue. At the upper end of the voice box are folds of tissue called the false vocal cords. Below them is another pair of folds that are the true vocal cords. They make sounds when air passes over them. The Adam's apple is a piece of cartilage on top of the larynx that causes a slight bulge in the neck.

Past the larynx is the trachea, a muscular tube held open by twenty horseshoe-shaped rings of cartilage, which can be felt through the skin of the neck. The trachea, which is only about four-and-one-half inches long, lies on top of the esophagus. Like the nose and throat, it is lined with ciliated mucous membranes. Any dust or debris that reaches the trachea

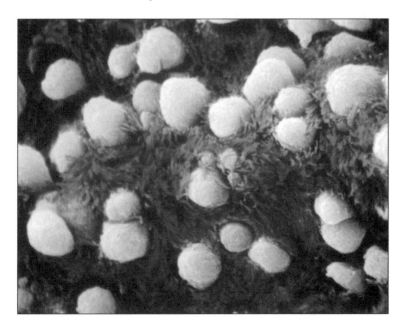

*Round, mucus-producing goblet cells cling to fine hairlike cilia in the bronchial passages of the human lung.*

is swept upward toward the mouth by the cilia. When the debris reaches the mouth, one of two things may happen. It can be swallowed and delivered to the stomach, where digestive juices destroy any bacteria that may be present. Or it can be expelled from the body with a sneeze or cough.

When the nose is clogged by nasal secretions, air must enter the body through the mouth. Whether it enters by mouth or nose, inhaled air travels down the throat from the pharynx through the larynx. From there it flows through the trachea, or windpipe, on its way to the lungs.

## The Lower Respiratory Tract

The trachea divides into two branches called the primary bronchi, one leading to each lung. The lungs are cone-shaped organs that fill most of the chest cavity. They have a spongy texture and are divided into distinct lobes. The right lung has three lobes, but the left lung, which shares space in the chest cavity with the heart, has only two. The upper tips of the lungs extend to the neck, just above the level of the collarbone. At their base, the lungs sit on a large sheet of muscle called the diaphragm.

Covering the lungs are two layers of pleural membranes. The pleura form a double sac around each lung. One pleural membrane sticks to the lungs, and the other lines the inside of the chest cavity. Lubricating fluid lies between them. The two pleural membranes are held close together by the cohesive force of pleural fluid, much as two pieces of glass are held together by a thin film of water. This fluid reduces friction, allowing the lungs to gently slide in the chest cavity as they expand and contract during breathing.

Each primary bronchus enters one lung. The right primary bronchus is shorter and slightly larger than the left. Therefore if a small object is inhaled, it usually enters the right bronchus. The primary bronchi divide into smaller secondary bronchi. Like limbs on a tree, these branch into still smaller tubes called segmented bronchi. Ten segmented bronchi or limbs are in the right lung and nine in the left lung. Each segmented bronchus carries air to an individual portion of the lung called

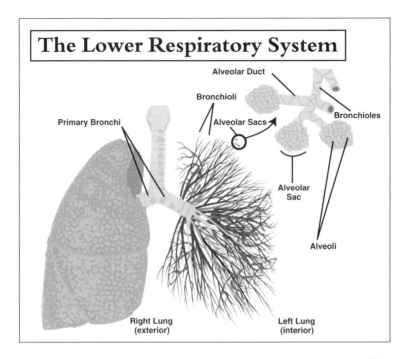

## The Lower Respiratory System

Alveolar Duct

Bronchioli

Alveolar Sacs

Bronchioles

Primary Bronchi

Alveolar Sac

Alveoli

Right Lung (exterior)

Left Lung (interior)

a segment. Segmentation in the lungs is very important. The membranes that divide one segment from another prevent infection from spreading quickly throughout the lungs.

The segmented bronchi continue to divide into smaller and smaller limbs or airways. They split at least twenty more times until they are reduced to tiny bronchioles that have a diameter of one millimeter. Each bronchiole further divides into minuscule alveolar ducts that might be compared to the twigs on trees. These have a diameter of only one-half millimeter. There are about 250,000 alveolar ducts in the lungs.

## Alveoli and Gas Exchange

Each alveolar duct ends in a group of tiny air sacs called alveoli, which look like little clusters of bubbles or grapes. Surrounding each cluster are minute blood vessels called capillaries. The close proximity of capillaries and alveoli allows gases to diffuse between these structures. Oxygen in the air sacs passes into the blood; in exchange, carbon dioxide in the blood flows into the air sacs. This exchange of gases between capillaries and alveoli is possible because the walls of each tiny air sac consist of a single layer of cells. Likewise, capillary walls are just one cell thick.

Gases move in predictable ways. Research has shown that gases always travel or diffuse from an area where they are highly concentrated to an area where they are less concentrated. Oxygen and carbon dioxide in the body follow this same behavior. After an inhalation, the alveoli have a higher concentration of oxygen and a lower concentration of carbon dioxide than the blood. So oxygen diffuses through the cell walls of the alveoli into the capillaries and enters the blood. Because carbon dioxide levels are higher in the blood than in the alveoli, carbon dioxide passes from the blood into the tiny air sacs. Immediately, the newly oxygenated blood begins its journey from the lungs to the left side of the heart. From there it is pumped to the entire body.

As blood delivers its oxygen to body cells carbon dioxide gas, a waste product of oxygen metabolism, diffuses out of body cells into the blood. Blood that has completed one circuit of the body then returns to the right side of the heart, which pumps it back to the lungs. At this point blood entering the capillaries of the lungs has a low concentration of oxygen and a high concentration of carbon dioxide. At the alveoli, blood deposits its new load of carbon dioxide and picks up another shipment of oxygen. The heart then pumps the oxygen-filled blood through the body again.

## Take a Deep Breath

Breathing is usually an automatic behavior; the respiratory center of the brain controls this activity without conscious instructions from the individual. The body monitors the amount of carbon dioxide and oxygen in the blood. When the blood contains too much carbon dioxide or too little oxygen, it becomes slightly acidic. Cells throughout the body constantly check blood acidity. When it is high, a signal is sent to the respiratory center of the brain to increase the intensity of breathing. By breathing faster and deeper, more oxygen enters the bloodstream, and more carbon dioxide is exhaled. Blood then loses its acidity and returns to its optimal neutral condition.

*A runner takes deep, quick breaths to maintain oxygen and carbon dioxide levels in his body.*

Physical activity affects how much oxygen is needed in the body. At rest, an adult inhales about one-fourth of a pint of air with each breath. When exercising, muscles and joints send messages to the brain to increase depth and speed of breathing. Consequently, volume increases to two pints of air with each breath. The body is finely tuned to deliver the same amount of oxygen to cells no matter what the level of activity. During exercise the amounts of oxygen and carbon dioxide in blood do not increase. Excess carbon dioxide produced by vigorous activity is exhaled as quickly as it is made.

Air moves in and out of the lungs for the same reason that any gas moves from one place to another: Gases naturally flow from an area of high concentration or pressure to one of low concentration or pressure. As the lungs change size, air pressure within them changes. When lungs are expanded, the air pressure in them is low. When they contract, air pressure rises.

Changes in lung size are caused by contraction and relaxation of chest muscles. The lungs and other chest organs are surrounded by a bony cage made up of the ribs, spine, and sternum or breast bone. These bones are supported by a system of muscles. The diaphragm, a large muscle at the base of the lungs, is instrumental in changing the size of the chest cavity and therefore the size of the lungs.

During an inhalation the diaphragm contracts and moves downward. At the same time, muscles between the ribs contract, expanding the sides of the chest cavity. The lungs now have room to expand downwards and sideways. This expansion increases the space or volume in the lungs. Due to this increase in lung volume air pressure within the lungs drops. Because air pressure outside the body is greater than inside the lungs, air rushes into the lungs. Air continues to flow into the lungs until the pressure inside the lungs is equal to the atmospheric pressure outside the body. At this point inhalation is complete.

## Breathe Out

Exhalation is a passive process. As the diaphragm and rib muscles relax they return to their original size, much like a stretched rubber band returns to its normal size when re-

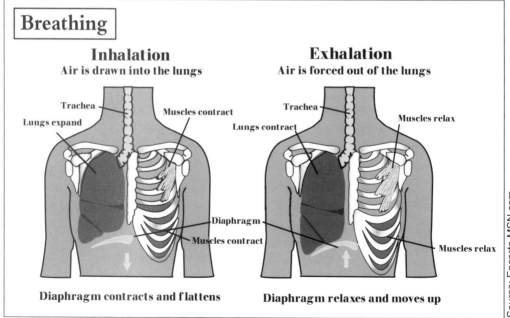

**Breathing**

### Inhalation
**Air is drawn into the lungs**

Trachea
Muscles contract
Lungs expand
Diaphragm
Muscles contract

**Diaphragm contracts and flattens**

### Exhalation
**Air is forced out of the lungs**

Trachea
Muscles relax
Lungs contract
Muscles relax

**Diaphragm relaxes and moves up**

Source: Encarta.MSN.com.

leased. This causes the space or volume inside the chest to decrease. Reduced space increases air pressure in the lungs, so air flows out the mouth and nose. Air continues to leave the lungs until pressure in the lungs is again equal to air pressure outside the body. When this happens, exhalation ends.

The contents of inspired air and expired air are not the same. As might be expected, expired air contains more carbon dioxide and less oxygen than inspired air. Air entering the lungs contains gases in the same proportion found in the atmosphere, namely 21 percent oxygen and 0.03 percent carbon dioxide. After gases are exchanged at the cellular level, air in the alveoli holds 14 percent oxygen and 5.5 percent carbon dioxide. The reasons for this difference in composition is that 7 percent of the oxygen in the air is transported to and absorbed by cells in the body; air returned to the lungs carries high levels of carbon dioxide produced by cells as a waste product of respiration.

Although the alveoli lose most of their "used" air during an exhalation, the lungs never completely empty. There is always about one-fifth of the lung's air capacity left in the alveoli. This residual volume prevents alveoli from collapsing and allows the exchange of gases to continue.

## The Blood Delivery System

Once oxygen has entered the blood it must be delivered to all cells in the body. Red blood cells are the primary carriers of oxygen. A teaspoon of blood contains more than 22 million red blood cells. Each cell is a tiny disk that is concave on both sides.

Blood carries oxygen in two ways: dissolved, and as parts of hemoglobin molecules. Fluids can hold only a limited amount of dissolved gases. Because blood cannot hold enough dissolved oxygen to meet the cells' needs, most of the oxygen that enters blood forms chemical bonds with a blood protein called hemoglobin. Hemoglobin increases the oxygen-carrying ability of blood forty-five times.

Every red blood cell contains about 300 million molecular units of gas-binding hemoglobin. Hemoglobin, a very

*The concave shape of these red blood cells maximizes the surface area over which the exchange of gases may take place.*

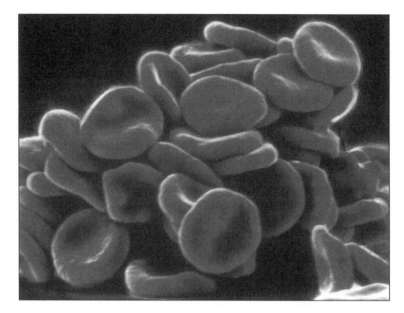

large molecule, has two components: heme and globin. Globin is a protein that is made up of four folded chains of molecules. Each chain surrounds one heme molecule. Heme contains iron, the element which gives red blood cells their characteristic color. The heme molecules of hemoglobin loosely bond with oxygen.

As newly oxygenated blood circuits the body, the oxygen leaves hemoglobin molecules and enters body cells. At the same time, carbon dioxide and water diffuse out of body cells into the bloodstream.

Carbon dioxide can be transported by the blood in three different ways. Like oxygen, a small amount of carbon dioxide dissolves in the fluid portion of the blood. An additional amount combines with hemoglobin, the oxygen-carrying molecule. Much of the carbon dioxide undergoes a chemical reaction to form bicarbonate ions that travel through blood. Bicarbonate ions play an important role in regulating the blood's level of acidity.

## Cellular Respiration: Making Energy

The purpose of all respiratory processes is to deliver oxygen to cells for cellular respiration. In each cell a simple sugar called glucose is converted to life-sustaining energy. This process can be compared to burning wood in a bonfire. In this analogy, glucose is the wood. Oxygen is needed to burn wood and it also is needed to break down glucose. A fire releases energy in the form of heat, whereas the breakdown of glucose in cells releases energy to sustain life. Just as there are wastes such as ashes and carbon dioxide produced by burning wood in a fire, respiration produces the waste products carbon dioxide and water.

## The Whole Story: The Role of The Respiratory System

Since earliest times, man has known that the act of breathing is associated with life. Even though the entire mechanics of breathing were not well understood until the last century, most people knew that when a body ceases to breathe, it is no longer alive. Through literature and music, the "breath of life" has been recognized for its life-giving role.

Breathing is a more complex act than a casual observer might imagine. The results of breathing extend far beyond the lungs to every cell in the body.

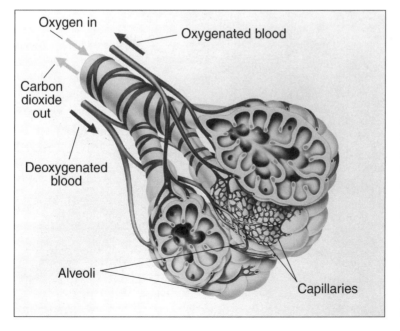

An illustration shows tiny capillaries that surround each alveolus. Deoxygenated blood enters the alveoli where it gives up its load of carbon dioxide and picks up oxygen. Therefore blood leaving the alveoli is freshly oxygenated.

Within the lungs, oxygen from inhaled air diffuses from the alveoli into the capillaries and enters the blood. The blood carries the oxygen to the body cells. Cells are individual living units. To remain alive each of them uses oxygen to change glucose into energy. This process produces two wastes: carbon dioxide and water. These wastes diffuse from the cells into the bloodstream, which carries them to the capillaries in the lungs. There they diffuse into lung tissues and are expelled by exhalation.

# 2 | Respiratory Events

Breathing is an automatic behavior. Without even thinking about it, most adults inhale fifteen to twenty-five times a minute. The respiratory system works around the clock to supply oxygen to body cells. Sometimes the respiratory system goes temporarily awry or springs into surprising action to protect the body. This can result in some unusual and interesting respiratory events.

## Sneezing

At the beginning of the respiratory tract are the nasal cavities and the mouth. Here one of the most common occurrences takes place, the sneeze. During a sneeze air and tiny droplets of liquid mucus are expelled from the mouth and nose. Each sneeze may contain over five thousand droplets. Sometimes these droplets carry germs that can transmit colds and other illnesses caused by bacteria. Sneezes can project these infected droplets up to twelve feet in distance. The expelled air from a sneeze has been clocked at an amazing 160 miles per hour.

   In the past, the intense release of air through a sneeze gave rise to an expression that has survived to present times, "God bless you." People used to think that the force of air expelled in a sneeze symbolized the soul fleeing the body, and they would say "God bless you" to keep devils from invading the body of a sneezer. Today, however, science has provided a straightforward explanation for this phenomenon.

A variety of irritants can settle in the mucous membranes of the nose and initiate a sneeze. Things such as dust and pollen bother the sensitive nasal passages. As the nerves in the nasal cavity become irritated, they send a message to the respiratory center at the base of the brain. The brain directs the muscles involved in respiration to react to the nuisance. The body responds by inhaling deeply and closing the airways. The respiratory muscles then squeeze the chest. As soon as the lungs are under high pressure, the airways suddenly open. Air in the lungs explodes upward and outward, carrying the irritants from the nose with it.

*By sneezing this woman expels thousands of tiny moisture droplets that carry irritants out of the nasal passage.*

# Coughing

Coughing is a lot like sneezing. The irritants that cause sneezing are in the nasal cavity, but those that produce coughs are located in the lower part of the respiratory tract. Coughing is a reflex action that occurs when sensory nerves of the trachea, larynx, or bronchi are stimulated. The act of coughing means that there is something in the respiratory tract that should not be there. A variety of irritants, including dust particles or phlegm from infection, can trigger coughing.

Coughing is a very important defense mechanism for the respiratory tract because it expels contaminants from the lungs and airways. If people could not cough, they would not be able to clear their airways and would develop respiratory problems. When dust and dirt invade these passageways, an environment forms that is perfect for bacterial growth. This can lead to a variety of respiratory infections and illnesses.

Just before a cough, air is inhaled deeply and then the larynx closes. Muscles in the abdomen and the chest contract, increasing the pressure in the lungs. As soon as the larynx reopens, air is projected at high speeds to clear dust, dirt, and other secretions from the airway. People with respiratory diseases sometimes have trouble coughing deeply because they cannot take in a good breath at the start of the process.

There are two main types of coughs: dry and productive. A dry cough is usually found in the early stages of diseases such as bronchitis, asthma, or pneumonia. Or it can be a result of food or other swallowed material that has become lodged in the airway. In the case of lodged material, the force of the dry cough will expel the substance blocking the airway.

Productive coughs generate a semisolid residue called phlegm. Such coughs are common in people that smoke tobacco products. In smokers, the airways are trying to expel the excess mucus that is produced as a result of smoking. No matter what the cause, the appearance of phlegm may provide clues about the underlying cause of the cough.

*The chronic cough experienced by most smokers results from nicotine and other contaminants in the lungs.*

Phlegm that is colorless may simply indicate irritation and generally does not require treatment. Coughs that produce large amounts of green, yellow, brown, or black phlegm signify a respiratory infection. For example, a cough filled with streaks of blood may signal the presence of a disease such as lung cancer, tuberculosis, or a lung abscess. A cough that produces phlegm that is frothy and pink means that red blood cells may be leaking into inflamed alveoli of the lungs. Such coughs call for immediate medical attention.

# Yawning

Another common occurrence in the respiratory tract is the yawn. Like coughing and sneezing, it involves a deep inhalation of air. Unlike coughing or sneezing, this inhalation takes place while the mouth is wide open. Scientists do not completely understand why people yawn. People yawn at all times of the day, while sitting, standing, jogging, and working. Clearly yawning is not necessarily a sign of boredom. However, it occurs often during times of exhaustion, stress, or sedentary activities.

It is known that yawning is an involuntary respiratory reflex that affects the amount of oxygen and carbon dioxide in the blood. The reflex is controlled by a section of the brain called the hypothalamus. One of the oldest and most respected explanations for yawning states that people yawn

*Though generally related to moments of inactivity, stress, or boredom, the reasons for yawning remain a mystery.*

when the lungs are low on oxygen. When at rest, breathing is shallow and only some of the alveoli of the lungs are put into use. When these air sacs do not get fresh air, they partially collapse. This collapse may prompt the brain to initiate either a sigh or a yawn to ventilate all the alveoli.

There are a few yawning acts that are common to everyone. When someone yawns, the head tilts back, the jaw drops, the eyes squint, and the brows wrinkle. Heart rate increases, an action that helps rid the body of excess carbon dioxide and bring more oxygen through blood vessels in the brain. Following a yawn, alertness is increased due to the uptake of oxygen.

One very interesting phenomenon is that unborn fetuses begin yawning about eleven weeks after conception. Since fetuses do not take oxygen into their lungs, it seems odd that they would need to yawn. It also is mysterious that yawning is contagious. Observing yawning can trigger a yawn. Humans begin to feel this contagious effect between the ages of one and two years old. Scientists have no proven explanation for this aspect of yawning. Some speculate it is a leftover social behavior from earlier human cultures; that at one time yawning may have signaled the beginning of an event, and other group members responded with a similar signal.

## Snoring

For many people, yawning precedes sleep. Sleep is a relaxing period when the body rests and gets ready for the next day. However, for one out of every seven adults, sleep is accompanied by snoring. When a person snores the uvula at the back of the throat and the soft palate vibrates with each passing breath. Gasping sounds accompany snoring because the tongue falls back in the throat and partially closes the windpipe. People who sleep on their backs with their mouths open are more prone to snore than people that sleep in other positions. In fact, historians report that in some cultures annoying buttons were sewn on the backs of nightclothes to prevent snorers from sleeping on their back. Snoring is more common in people who have colds, enlarged tonsils, inflamed nasal polyps, or loose dentures. People that are overweight or have nasal congestion are likely to snore. Snoring is not dangerous, but it can signal a more serious condition called sleep apnea.

## Sleep Apnea

Some people snore, pause before the next breath, then gasp for air. When breathing stops for ten seconds or more, the condition is called sleep apnea. People with this disorder unintentionally hold their breath while they sleep. Each time breathing stops the oxygen level in the blood falls, and the heart has to compensate by doing extra work. This makes blood pressure climb, and heart rhythms can become irregular. The continuous fall of oxygen in the blood signals the diaphragm and chest to contract to bring air into the lungs. Gasping for air, the sleeper is briefly jarred awake, takes a deep breath, and falls asleep again. This pattern of sleeping, holding breath, gasping, and waking occurs all during the night. Consequently, people with sleep apnea get very little rest. They start each new day feeling tired and groggy.

*Wires attached to the nose, mouth, heart, brain, and eyes test the effect of respiratory function on sleep patterns.*

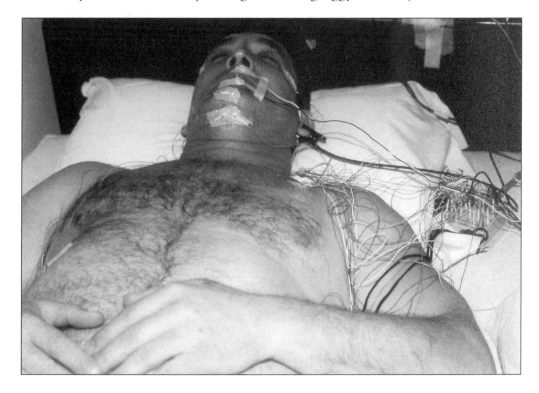

Sleep apnea can be caused by either an obstruction of the airway or a nervous system disorder. Obstructive sleep apnea is the most common type in middle-aged, overweight males. The cause can be as simple as a fatty neck that closes down on the trachea when the person reclines during sleep. It can also be caused by a relaxation of muscles located at the back of the throat. The tissue surrounding these malfunctioning muscles blocks off the airway and stops intake of air. Enlarged tonsils can also produce obstructive sleep apnea.

Neurological disorders can result in a version of this malfunction called central sleep apnea. People with this condition may not inhale for a while, but then inhale suddenly and rapidly. Some people with central sleep apnea inhale regularly, but have trouble exhaling because their muscles relax at a moment when they should be active. In either case, in central sleep apnea the body simply forgets to breathe. This cessation of breathing can last for as little as a few seconds up to as long as two minutes.

## Help for Those Who Gasp for Breath

People who develop the disturbing symptoms of sleep apnea may go to a sleep lab to be monitored. While clients are asleep scientists measure oxygen in their blood and the airflow through their mouth and nose. Brain waves, heart rate, and eye movements are monitored. People found to have obstructive sleep apnea are sometimes fitted with a special mask that is hooked to an air compressor at bedtime. This arrangement provides constant air pressure to keep the airway open. Some simpler treatments for sleep apnea are to reduce antihistamine and sleeping pill consumption at bedtime. These medications tend to relax the muscles of the upper airway. In overweight individuals, weight loss also helps correct some cases of obstructive sleep apnea. There are medications available to reduce snoring and to stimulate the throat muscles to prevent airway collapse.

## Hiccups

Another respiratory-related phenomenon is hiccups. Like snoring, hiccupping involves the nose and mouth, but it has

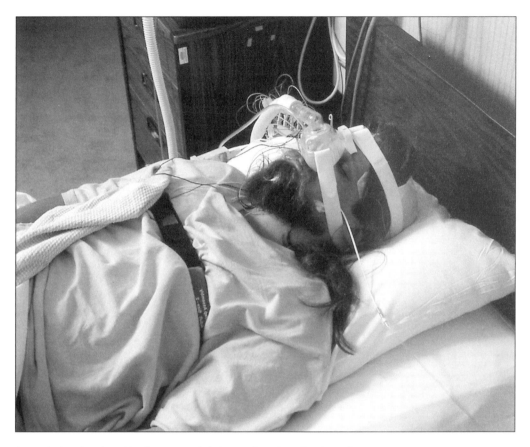

its origins in the diaphragm. A hiccup begins during the act of inhalation. The diaphragm pulls down as if preparing to take a deep breath. For some reason the nerves that serve this large muscle become irritated and the diaphragm contracts involuntarily. The diaphragm, which usually moves in a rhythmic pattern, spasms into erratic contractions. Breathing becomes irregular as the person takes large gulps of air. When air fills the lungs, the brain sends an urgent message to the throat to limit the further intake of air. In a matter of milliseconds a signal causes the glottis to rapidly close. This prevents air from actually going into the lungs. These mixed messages result in the weird "hic" sound that is produced as air hits the vocal cords of the closed glottis with each jerky movement of the diaphragm. When the diaphragm settles back into a normal rhythm, the hiccups stop.

*A Stanford University lab monitors a patient with acute sleep apnea while he sleeps.*

Scientists do not know why people hiccup since it serves no useful function in the body. Hiccuping does occur during fetal development, perhaps as a way to develop strength in the inspiratory muscles that will be put into use immediately after birth. In adults, hiccups may be leftover reflexes. Even though scientists cannot pinpoint the reason behind hiccupping, they do know that certain activities in adults can trigger it; for example, drinking or eating too much. In this case it is thought that distention of the stomach may irritate the diaphragm and cause it to spasm. Most people hiccup for only a few minutes, but there are people who hiccup non-stop for years at a time.

No matter what the cause, treatments to help stop hiccups vary greatly. Some well-meaning individuals try to scare the victim. Many people drink large quantities of water or hold their breath. Everyone reacts differently to treatments. The goal of any hiccup-stopping technique is to interrupt the abnormal rhythm of the diaphragm by reducing the oxygen supply, increasing the amount of carbon dioxide, or tricking the nervous system.

## Hyperventilation: Air Hunger

Like hiccupping, hyperventilation involves abnormal inspirations. In hyperventilation, breathing is faster than normal because the body mistakenly feels like it cannot get enough air. As a result the person breathes too much. The fast breathing that is characteristic of hyperventilation creates problems by causing an excessive amount of carbon dioxide to be exhaled. In turn, carbon dioxide levels in the blood and brain drop too low. Low carbon dioxide levels cause arteries going to the brain to constrict, reducing blood flow throughout the body. When this occurs, a person experiences a shortage of oxygen that triggers feelings of anxiety, irritability, and confusion. Also, reduced carbon dioxide can cause respiratory alkalosis, a condition in which blood acidity is lowered. It results in dizziness and tingling in the hands, feet, and lips.

Anxiety or fear can bring about hyperventilation. Diseases such as asthma can also cause this malfunction in breathing. Normally people inhale somewhere between 0.88 and 1.3 gallons of air each minute. People with asthma who are hyperventilating may gulp an amazing 2.2 to 3.0 gallons of air each minute. People who are hyperventilating take much of their air in orally rather than through the nose. Even though hyperventilation is scary, it is not usually dangerous. The best way to prevent such an episode is by avoiding situations and activities that cause anxiety. After an episode of hyperventilation begins, deep breathing into a paper bag placed over the mouth and nose can sometimes stop it. After breathing slowly into the bag ten to fifteen times, the bag is removed. If breathing is not back to normal, the treatment can be repeated until symptoms subside. It is helpful for people who are hyperventilating to try to remain calm and make a conscious effort to breathe slowly.

*A young girl struggles to breathe during an asthma attack.*

## The Spectrum of Respiratory Events

Because the respiratory system begins with structures in the face, its events are well known to most people. Scientists understand the biology behind some of these events better than they do others. For example, coughing and sneezing are normal mechanisms for removing irritants from the upper respiratory passages. It is easy to understand how they help the body by clearing out dust, dirt, and germs from sensitive mucous membranes of the nose and throat. Scientists also know that snoring, a sound produced by some people while they sleep, is caused by the vibration of soft tissue in the nose and throat. Even some of the causes of sleep apnea, a serious condition in which the sleeper stops breathing, are understood.

*Coughing is one of the more obvious functions of the respiratory system.*

On the other hand, there are several respiratory events that everyone has experienced but which few can explain. The most common may be yawning, which researchers believe may be related to the need for increasing oxygen levels in the body when it is at rest. Hiccuping, a temporary problem caused by spastic contractions of the diaphragm, is another mystery. Its function, if any, is not clear. Some people occasionally experience an attack of hyperventilation. For some unknown reason their respiratory systems mistakenly act as if their bodies are low on oxygen. By studying all respiratory events, especially those that are poorly understood, scientists can better decipher the normal functions of the respiratory system.

# 3 Extreme Conditions

Most people don't think about breathing. Unless the act of inhaling and exhaling becomes difficult, breathing is a subconscious act. Under normal conditions plenty of oxygen is available to meet the body's needs, and breathing is comfortable. But under extreme conditions the normal functions of the respiratory system may be impaired. Changes in the environment, such as extreme fluctuations in air pressure, can stress the respiratory system and put it off balance. In response, the body attempts to correct these imbalances. Many times it does so effectively, but there are occasions where appropriate balance cannot be regained.

Two situations that challenge the respiratory system are traveling to high altitudes and underwater diving. In both circumstances the amount of pressure on the lungs changes dramatically. Generally the lungs only deal with atmospheric pressure. Atmospheric pressure is the weight of air pressing down on the earth. It determines how much air is pushed into the lungs with each breath. At sea level atmospheric pressure is 760 mmHg. This means that air presses down on a barometer with enough weight to support a column of mercury 760 millimeters (almost 3 inches) high. This is the air pressure at which the body functions most efficiently. Humans can survive at higher or lower pressures; however, problems develop when changes in pressure are extreme or when they occur rapidly.

# The Stresses of Mountain Climbing

Mountain climbing can have profound effects on the respiratory system. At twelve thousand feet above sea level, air pressure is less than half what it is at sea level; and the higher a mountaineer climbs, the greater the decrease in air pressure. Moreover, at twelve thousand feet air holds 40 percent fewer oxygen molecules than at the shore. In other words, there is not as much oxygen available to the respiratory system at high altitudes.

Although the composition of atmospheric air is the same at the shore as it is at twelve thousand feet and at twenty-nine thousand feet (the summit of Mount Everest), at high altitudes the number of air molecules in a given volume is low.

*Mountain climbers contend with depleted oxygen levels as they ascend to high altitudes.*

That is, air molecules are farther apart at high altitudes and air is less dense, or "thinner." And since there are fewer air molecules available at high altitudes than at low altitudes, mountain climbers draw in a smaller number of oxygen molecules with each breath than they would at sea level.

Because oxygen molecules are scarcer at high altitudes and because the air pressure is lower as well, oxygen does not pass easily from a climber's lungs to the blood. To compensate, the body works harder by increasing the rate of breathing, which is tiring and drains the body of energy. This is an important consideration in a physical activity as strenuous as mountain climbing. The conditions of low oxygen and air pressure cause serious health problems for some climbers.

## Oxygen Deprivation at High Altitudes

Hypoxia is any condition in which body tissues do not receive enough oxygen. It can occur when traveling to high elevations. The symptoms of hypoxia vary in severity from person to person; as altitude increases, symptoms usually increase. For many people the first indication of hypoxia is an inability to perform simple activities such as walking up a few steps of a stairway. Oxygen deprivation can occur anywhere above sea level, but most people do not really feel the effects until they reach an altitude of sixty-five hundred feet. People who are not accustomed to high elevations are more vulnerable to hypoxia than people who frequently visit high altitudes. In 1968 the Summer Olympics were held in Mexico City, seventy-three hundred feet above sea level. This location was a disadvantage to competitors who lived at low altitudes. Four of the five endurance track events were won by men who were accustomed to high altitudes because they had lived and trained for many years in mountainous regions.

## Acute Mountain Sickness

At sixty-five hundred feet and above, hypoxia is commonly referred to as acute mountain sickness (AMS). Rapid ascent to this height or higher can bring on some form of

AMS as the heart rate increases to send more blood to the lungs. This causes blood pressure to rise. When blood pressure is very high, some blood seeps into the alveoli of the lungs causing symptoms such as loss of appetite, headache, fatigue, shortness of breath, nausea, fuzzy thinking, and sleep disturbances. During sleep those who experience AMS may have stages of deep breathing followed by brief periods of apnea. Physical exertion usually worsens the symptoms. After a couple of days at high altitude, AMS symptoms diminish as the body adjusts to the new heights. If symptoms do not go away in three days the traveler is usually advised to descend to a lower altitude.

## Life-Threatening Mountain Sickness

At eight thousand feet and above, some people develop a more serious form of AMS called high-altitude pulmonary edema (HAPE). In this condition fluids begin to accumulate in the tissues of the lungs. Normally the network of vessels called the lymph system rapidly drains fluid from the lungs. But in HAPE, fluid accumulates faster than the lymph system can handle it. Fluids cause the alveoli of the lungs to swell and the pressure in pulmonary arteries to increase. As

*Doctors treat a man suffering from high-altitude pulmonary edema (HAPE).*

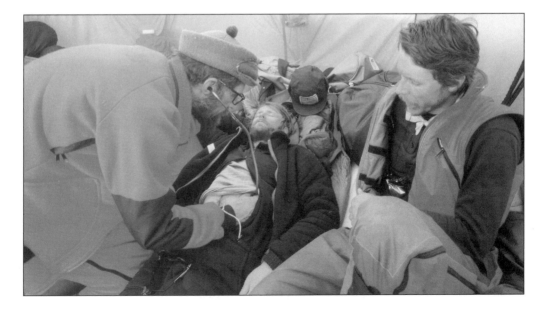

*A tube-shaped, portable pressure chamber called a Gamow bag is used to treat high-altitude cerebral edema (HACE).*

a result the HAPE sufferer feels short of breath. Other symptoms of HAPE are cyanosis, or blue coloration of the skin, and a cough that is accompanied by the expulsion of frothy pink sputum. Gurgling sounds caused by excess fluid in the lungs can be heard in the chest cavity. HAPE is five times more common in men than women. It is also more common in people that have had a previous episode of this condition, and in people that are already suffering from a respiratory infection such as a cold or bronchitis.

Without treatment, HAPE progresses into a very serious illness called high altitude cerebral edema (HACE). This disorder is not often seen at heights below ten thousand feet. In HACE the body responds to oxygen deprivation by diverting blood flow to the brain. High volumes of blood in the brain cause leakage of blood from the vessels into brain tissue. Swelling of the brain can result. The earliest symptoms of HACE are related to motor instability, and they include staggering, stumbling, confusion, and hallucinations. If not treated promptly a person may lapse into a coma and die.

A person suffering from HACE or HAPE should be moved to a lower altitude immediately but gradually. Upon arrival they may require supplements of oxygen and fluids. If transportation to a lower altitude is not possible, the climber can be placed in a pressurized chamber that gradually lowers the atmospheric pressure. A portable version of this chamber is called a Gamow bag. It weighs about fourteen pounds, so it is light enough to carry up a mountain as part of a mountaineering team's gear. In a medical emergency, the bag is pumped full of air that is high in oxygen to simulate conditions of a lower altitude. The person suffering from oxygen deprivation is placed in the inflated bag where the environment is similar to atmospheric conditions three thousand to five thousand feet below their actual location. After an hour or two the HAPE victim's body chemistry adjusts to this perceived "lower" elevation and symptoms abate. The sensation of being at a lower altitude lasts for about twelve hours. At this point the sick person exits the bag, and the party resumes the descent. Unfortunately some people have long-term effects from HAPE and HACE. Even after their apparent recovery they may experience difficulty with simple tasks of memorization, spelling, pronunciation, multiplying, and following directions.

## The Body Adjusts to High Altitudes

For most people the respiratory system functions without problems at high altitudes. Given some time the majority of the population can easily adjust to heights of ten thousand feet above sea level. The process of adapting to high altitude living is called acclimation. It occurs over a period of days or weeks. If people were not able to acclimate, there would be few vacationers traveling to places such as Aspen (7,850 feet) or Vail, Colorado (8,120 feet). Because the body can make amazing adjustments, people work and play in mountaineous areas.

Acclimation is a process. When the body is first exposed to high altitude and low air pressure, it responds by increasing the breathing and heart rates. This response immediately boosts the airflow through the alveoli of the lungs by about 60 percent. As airflow increases, the amount of oxygen that the body takes in also increases. The pulse and blood pressure rise sharply as the body strains to get oxygen to the cells. Increased blood pressure in pulmonary arteries forces blood into sections of the lungs that are rarely used at sea level. Eventually the lungs increase in size and therefore expose more alveolar surface area for the exchange of gases. After a few weeks bone marrow responds to the need for oxygen by making more red blood cells. More red blood cells in circulation mean that more oxygen can be transported through the body. The body also produces enzymes that accelerate the rate at which oxygen is transported from the red blood cells to the tissues. As a result, if a traveler remains at a high altitude for several weeks, airflow improves by an amazing 700 percent.

## Adapting to High Altitudes

People that stay at high altitudes for weeks, months, or years do become acclimated to the low pressure and to low oxygen levels. Once their bodies have adapted they can travel to even greater heights, as long as they ascend slowly so the body has plenty of time to acclimate to the lower air pressure at each new altitude. Slow ascent prevents altitude sicknesses. The body is not designed to adjust quickly to extreme changes in altitude. For example, if a person were flown in a helicopter from a town at sea level and lowered by ropes onto the summit of Mount Everest, death from hypoxia would result in

about an hour. Yet, hundreds of people have climbed to the top of Mount Everest and returned. One critical factor in their success was a slow ascent that allowed their bodies to acclimate to the increasing heights.

Some athletes who normally train at low altitudes take advantage of the body's adaptive behavior by practicing a technique called blood packing. These athletes travel to high altitudes and remain there to train. During the training period their lungs expand and their bone marrow produces extra red blood cells. Once they are acclimated and have reached prime condition, the athletes have a physician withdraw and store some of their blood, which is now superoxygenated. Just before a competition at a low altitude event, they have a transfusion of their own blood with the complement of extra red blood cells. This improves the athletes' strength and endurance during competitive events.

*Two climbers ascend slowly up the face of Mount Everest, giving their bodies time to adapt to the lowered air pressure.*

Olympic and professional sports officials discourage blood packing for two reasons: It gives an athlete an unfair advantage, and it can be dangerous. Because there is not a way to test athletes to determine if some are using blood packing, a ban on the practice cannot be enforced. Athletes are simply asked not to use this technique, and they are expected to honor the request. The dangerous side effects of the practice keep some people from trying it. Superoxygenated blood that is transfused into an athlete who is ready to perform causes that athlete's blood to be thicker than normal. Thickened blood is difficult for the heart to pump. Consequently, cardiac output is reduced and blood flow to muscles is reduced. Instead of experiencing the benefits of high levels of oxygen in muscles and prolonged endurance, the athlete may actually suffer from the opposite: low oxygen levels in the muscles and weakened endurance.

The human body is capable of adapting to very stressful conditions. People who live at high altitudes have some built-in adaptations that help them get plenty of oxygen. Highlanders are born with more alveoli and lung capillaries than lowlanders. People who live three miles up in the Andes or the Himalayan Mountains have more oxygen-carrying hemoglobin in their blood and greater lung capacity than people at lower altitudes.

In children born at high altitudes the oxygen transport systems develop quickly, often at the expense of body size. Consequently, many highland children are short. At high altitudes the metabolism of a fetus is geared to saving energy and conserving oxygen. The little bit of oxygen that is available is allocated mainly to vital organs, with the result that the muscles, skin, and bones receive less than normal amounts. Such babies have a low birth weight. For these reasons expectant highland mothers often travel to lower altitudes prior to giving birth, and they remain there for a year after delivery to boost their babies' chances of developing robust muscles, bones, and respiratory systems. Even so, on average, highland children are 0.3 to 1.5 inches shorter than lowland children.

# Breathing Underwater

High altitudes and low air pressure are not the only circumstances that stress the respiratory system. Traveling below sea level into the depths of the ocean presents the body with an entirely different set of challenges. As one dives underwater, pressure on the body increases. At a depth of thirty-three feet a diver experiences twice the pressure on the body that exists for the same person at sea level. Water is much heavier than air so it is not necessary to dive very deep to feel the effects of high water pressure. The deeper a person dives, of course, the greater the pressure.

Scuba (self-contained underwater breathing apparatus) divers breathe highly compressed air from tanks strapped to their backs. Scuba gear includes a regulator to insure that air is supplied to the diver's lungs at a pressure equal to the pressure of water on the diver's chest. If air pressure in the tank was not as high as water pressure on the body, air could not flow out of the tank, and the diver would be deprived of oxygen.

*A diver's tank delivers a mixture of gases nearly identical to those found in the air.*

# Raptures of the Deep

The gases in a scuba tank, usually nitrogen, oxygen, and carbon dioxide, are almost identical to those in atmospheric air. Although oxygen is the only gas divers really need, they cannot breathe pure oxygen because it generates harmful particles called free radicals. The presence of these free radicals in the body can cause severe nervous system disturbances, coma, and even death.

The nitrogen that comprises the majority of atmospheric air has no effect on the human body at sea level and at high altitudes. But under the ocean nitrogen can present a problem. Divers who descend to one hundred feet or deeper experience unique difficulties. At this depth they are inhaling air at four or five times the normal pressure. The behavior of nitrogen gas in the air is a concern because it becomes very soluble, or able to dissolve, at this pressure. Consequently, nitrogen gas does something that it doesn't do in the bodies of people on shore; it dissolves in the blood. Once dissolved, nitrogen finds its way to fatty tissues all over the body such as in the nervous system and bone marrow, and concentrates there. The accumulation of nitrogen in the nervous system can lead to serious problems because it affects the brain and slows cell communication. This may impair thinking, reaction time, and judgment of a diver. Divers whose blood levels are high in nitrogen suffer from a state of confusion called nitrogen narcosis. Because some have likened this condition to intoxication, it is also called "rapture of the deep." Symptoms of nitrogen narcosis dissipate as a diver ascends; at a depth of sixty feet most symptoms disappear. Unfortunately, some divers have drowned due to nitrogen narcosis. They became so confused that they swam deeper rather than back toward the surface, or they removed their scuba gear. To be safe, specialists recommend that recreational scuba divers stay above sixty feet. Commercial divers who must habitually work at depths below one hundred feet always work in pairs or groups so that anyone who gets in trouble can be moved to a safer depth.

*Deep-sea divers ascend slowly to avoid getting "the bends."*

## Diving and the Bends

Early in their training, divers are taught to ascend slowly. A diver who attempts to ascend quickly is at risk for decompression illness or "the bends." Because this can be a painful condition, divers who suffer from it are often bent over in agony. To understand why this danger exists, recall that at high pressure, nitrogen and other gases easily dissolve in liquids. That is why fizzy soft drinks, which contain pressurized carbon dioxide, are sold in tightly sealed cans or bottles. As long as the cap is on the bottle, pressure remains high and the carbon dioxide stays in solution. However, when the cap is removed pressure in the bottle immediately drops. At the lower pressure carbon dioxide comes out of solution and forms bubbles in the soft drink. In a similar way, gas dissolves in a diver's blood under high pressure. When the pressure is suddenly reduced, the gas can come out of solution and form dangerous bubbles in the blood.

Similarly, during an ascent from thirty feet or deeper, pressure on the diver's body decreases and nitrogen that was dissolved in the blood forms gas bubbles. In a slow ascent nitrogen bubbles enter the blood gradually and are carried to the lungs by the bloodstream. From the lungs, nitrogen is transferred from the capillaries to the alveoli, then is exhaled. However, if the ascent is fast, the diver's system cannot accommodate the sudden overload of nitrogen bubbles. Instead, bubbles in the blood get trapped in small veins, arteries, and body tissues. The bubbles are carried by the blood to different parts of the body where they cause problems in the tissues that receive them. They produce pain because they block the normal exchange of nutrients and oxygen, allowing waste products to accumulate.

Symptoms of the painful "bends" vary depending on where the nitrogen bubbles accumulate in the body. The effects can be mild or severe. Nausea, dizziness, pain in the joints, mood changes, numbness, skin rashes, coughing, shock, seizures, and even death can result after rapid ascent from deep water to the surface. If bubbles block the arteries leading to the spinal cord they cause paralysis; if they block those to the brain, stroke can result. If a great number of the bubbles go to the lungs, capillaries covering the alveoli may become congested. This restricts blood flow to the lungs and starves the diver of air. Symptoms of "the bends" can occur immediately upon resurfacing or even up to thirty-six hours later.

Divers avoid "the bends" by ascending slowly. During a slow ascent nitrogen gas is carried by the blood to the lungs, where it is exhaled. Divers learn this from good training and knowledge of diving safety. If forced to surface quickly by an injury or other emergency, a diver should be rushed to the nearest decompression chamber. Once the victim is in the chamber, high pressure conditions like those of deep water are recreated. The pressure is then gradually lowered to simulate a slow ascent. This gives the body an opportunity to process nitrogen as it comes out of solution in the blood.

## Diving and Ruptured Lungs

The "bends" are not the only risk facing divers during their swim to the surface. Since pressure on a diver drops as the diver swims toward the surface, ascent must be slow. Fast ascent from deep water can result in ruptured lungs. Most divers unconsciously take a deep breath before they begin their ascent. On the way up they must continue to inhale and exhale so the pressure inside and outside their bodies will equalize. When divers hold their breath and ascend without exhaling, air held in the lungs expands rapidly. This expansion can cause a lung to rupture or burst. When this happens, the diver's life is in danger.

*A diver is quickly stripped of his wetsuit and tank to enter a decompression chamber aboard a ship.*

Loss of a functioning lung can be disasterous. With only one lung to absorb oxygen from the compressed air, a diver's oxygen level drops immediately. This means that little oxygen is available for the brain. In addition, blood and body fluids from the rupture block airways. As a result the diver may lose consciousness and drown. If the diver is lucky enough to make it to the surface, he or she will cough up blood and need medical attention as quickly as possible to repair the damaged organ. Divers can avoid this life-threatening injury by making an effort to inhale and exhale when surfacing. The golden rule of Scuba diving is "never hold your breath." Most of the divers who have suffered a burst lung did so because their equipment malfunctioned and they were forced to ascend from deep water at an unsafe speed.

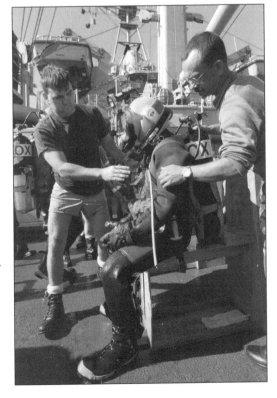

Japanese pearl divers go to risky depths without air tanks.

## Breath Hold Divers Have Unique Challenges

Breath hold divers, including swimmers, pearl divers, and coral divers, do not carry air tanks; they simply hold their breath underwater. Those who reach a depth of thirty-three feet or more are impacted by pressure changes. At thirty-three feet, the pressure from water surrounding the body shrinks lungs to one-half their normal size. At this depth the pressure of water is twice as strong as air pressure. As a diver swims back to the surface pressure lessens, allowing air in the lungs to expand and to return lungs to their normal size.

A serious respiratory danger for breath hold divers is shallow-water blackout, loss of consciousness just before reaching the surface of the water. This occurs when divers try to hold their breath too long. Normally, when people on land or underwater hold their breath, the amount of carbon dioxide in the blood increases as the amount of oxygen decreases. The buildup of carbon dioxide is a safety mechanism that triggers a hunger for air and an urgent need to breathe. The need to breathe causes people on land to gasp, and it signals divers that it is time to swim quickly to the surface.

Some competitive and experienced divers participate in events that require them to hold their breath for as long as three or four minutes. To stay under so long, they must fight their natural tendency to surface when they first feel the need to breathe. To give themselves more time underwater, some use a dangerous technique that delays the need to breathe. Unfortunately, the technique, called hyperventilation, can have fatal consequences if the divers' oxygen levels drop low enough to cause loss of consciousness.

Hyperventilation in diving serves to extend the amount of time a diver can stay underwater. Those who employ this very risky deep-breathing technique start by blowing off or exhaling a large amount of the carbon dioxide in their body. The logic behind this practice is to start the dive with abnormally low levels of carbon dioxide. This prevents carbon dioxide from building up to levels that trigger the need to breathe while the diver is underwater. In other words, with low carbon dioxide levels the sensation to breathe is delayed and the diver can stay underwater without feeling an urgency to surface. To use this technique divers must know exactly how long their bodies can function while they hold their breath, and they must time themselves while underwater. If the diver inadvertently stays under too long, oxygen levels drop so low that the diver passes out and drowns. Hyperventilation prior to diving is an unsafe practice.

## Essential Knowledge for Mountaineers and Divers

Athletes often know more about their respiratory systems than the average man or woman on the street. To enjoy the sports of mountain climbing and diving, they must be familiar with dangers that can result from extreme fluctuations in pressure and from lack of oxygen in their bodies. Knowledge about the respiratory system and how it delivers oxygen to cells can mean the difference between success and failure, or even life and death. Learning what it takes for the body to accommodate itself to extreme conditions is a must.

*Knowing the mechanics of the respiratory system can be as critical to a climber's survival as proper climbing gear.*

Experienced mountaineers know the value of acclimating to increasing altitudes. Instead of forging to the top of mountain peaks, wise climbers establish camps or resting stations along the way to give their bodies time to adapt to lower atmospheric oxygen levels and pressure. By doing so they maintain enough oxygen to support all their body systems. Consequently, their bodies generate the energy needed for the difficult task of climbing, and their brains have enough oxygen to make wise decisions.

Like mountain climbers, divers are trained to pay attention to pressure changes. Whereas climbers deal with very low pressure, divers must contend with high pressure on their bodies due to the weight of water. High pressure collapses the lungs and forces gases to dissolve in blood. Wise divers learn all the safety rules of deep water travel.

# Diseases of the Respiratory System

The respiratory system opens directly to the environment through the mouth and nose. Airborne particles loaded with infectious agents have access to respiratory organs with every breath. Even though respiratory openings are protected with tissues specialized for defense, the system is nevertheless exposed to a host of disease-causing agents. If a disease-causing organism does get past the body's defenses, it can cause infection. Respiratory illnesses can be as mild as a day or two of the sniffles, or as severe as pneumonia. In many cases respiratory tissues respond to illness by swelling and releasing mucus. Consequently, most respiratory ailments have similar symptoms such as runny nose, stuffy head, congestion, and fever. These symptoms vary in intensity, depending on their cause.

## No Cure for the Common Cold

One of the best known disorders of the respiratory tract is the common cold. Its symptoms include a stuffy head, runny nose, low-grade fever, cough, mild body aches, and watery eyes. These symptoms occur because the mucous membranes that line the upper respiratory tract become swollen, narrowing the passageways of the respiratory tract. Mucous glands respond to inflammation by secreting large amounts of fluid. Symptoms usually begin from one to three days after infection with a cold-causing virus. Coughing may continue for more than a week.

Colds are very contagious. They can be spread from one person to another through infected droplets sprayed in the air by coughing and sneezing. But the most common way to spread a cold is through hand-to-hand contact. If there are viral secretions on an infected person's hand, his or her cold can be spread by touching other people. That is why hands should be washed often during the cold season. Many believe that sleeping in a drafty room or getting wet in a rainstorm causes colds. This is not true. Viruses cause colds, not the weather conditions. However, environmental factors can sometimes lower the body's resistance to infection. Research shows that it is easier for people to catch colds when they are fatigued, stressed, or experiencing allergic reactions to conditions around them.

There is no cure for the common cold. Symptoms continue until the body's immune system is strong enough to defeat the virus. Although some illnesses confer immunity to

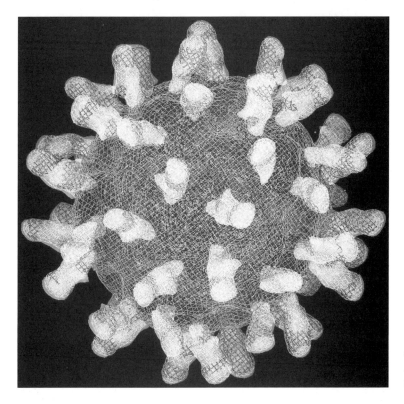

*A computer-simulated model of the cold virus.*

those who survive a single attack, very little protection against future colds is gained by infection with any single cold virus. Consequently, people can catch colds repeatedly. This is because there are many different strains of the cold virus, and the body cannot build up an immunity to every strain.

Doctors can usually diagnose a cold from a description of its symptoms. Sometimes a cold can mimic other conditions, like allergic reactions. Treatment for colds includes rest and plenty of fluids. Fluids prevent the secretions that accumulate in airways from hardening and blocking passage of air; rest allows the body's immune system to destroy disease-causing viruses and to repair damaged tissues. Good hygiene and frequent hand washing can lessen the likelihood of catching another cold.

The common cold can develop into more serious conditions if bacteria sneak into the body as secondary invaders. When the body is fighting a cold its resistance to other infections is lowered. Bacteria can invade the nearby sinus cavities or the trachea, causing infection and inflammation in these areas. When this happens symptoms get worse. Nasal secretions change from watery to thick, and fever may rise.

## Influenza

Like the common cold, influenza (the flu) is caused by a virus. And like the cold, the flu is caused by many different viral strains. Flu symptoms are more severe than cold symptoms. They include a high fever, runny nose, cough, headache, malaise, body aches, inflamed nasal and airway passages, and scratchy throat. Bouts with the influenza virus often put people in bed for a few days. A person will experience the first symptoms anywhere from twenty-four to forty-eight hours after infection. The flu usually makes its presence known with chills and fever. After a few days the fever may spike up to 103°F. Body aches with the flu are much worse than those of a cold, and some people also suffer from nausea and vomiting. The headache associated with the flu feels like it originates behind the eyes, and bright light makes it worse. For most people fever lasts

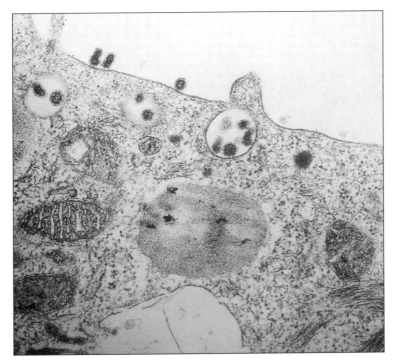

*An influenza virus, shown as light-colored bubbles with black spots, penetrates a human cell.*

only five days, but the cough may persist for several weeks. Some people may take as long as six weeks to recover from the weakness and fatigue that accompanies the infection.

Influenza is very contagious. Coughing and sneezing can transmit the virus by spreading infecting droplets in the air. But like the common cold, this virus is most likely to be spread by touching the hands of an infected person. There is no cure for influenza. Once exposed to a certain strain of flu virus, the body makes antibodies to protect against re-infection with that particular strain. As a rule, however, the viral strain responsible for most cases of the flu changes from year to year. In any event, there are so many strains of flu viruses that no attempt is made to develop vaccines against all of them. Each year scientists called epidemiologists predict which strain is most likely to enter a certain area of the country. A vaccine is made against that strain and offered to people who wish to take it. A vaccination is the best way to avoid getting the flu, but it is by no means a guarantee. Older people and people with chronic illnesses for whom influenza can

*A flu vaccine can provide protection against only the virus strain for which it was developed.*

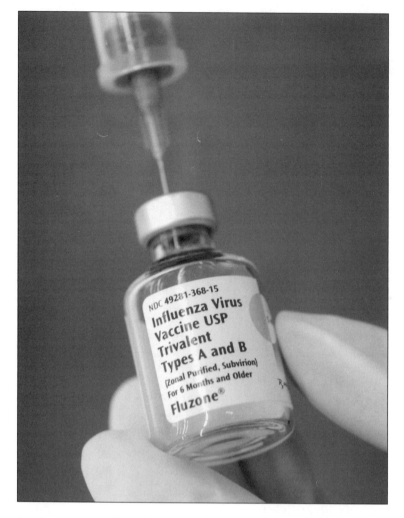

be fatal are usually advised to take the influenza vaccine. The vaccine is available in early autumn so the body has time to produce antibodies that will be at their peak during flu season.

Doctors can usually diagnose the flu from its symptoms and their knowledge of epidemics in the area. In cases where there is a question about diagnosis, respiratory secretions can be examined for viral particles. Bed rest and fluids are recommended during recovery. Drugs that contain acetaminophen or ibuprofen may be used to reduce high fever. Patients are advised to avoid all forms of physical exertion until the body temperature has been back to normal for at least forty-eight hours. By resting, the body can devote most of its energy to destroying viruses and repairing tissue damage.

As with the common cold, bacterial infections can sometimes accompany influenza. Bacteria can easily invade the respiratory tract during this time because the flu virus destroys the tract's epithelium cells. These cells must be in good condition to mount a defense against invading germs. When bacteria invade the respiratory tract during the flu, doctors may administer antibiotics to fight the infection.

## Sinusitis

The nasal sinuses are spaces within the skull bones. Their proximity to the airways makes them vulnerable to infection. Infections of the sinuses can be caused by bacteria,

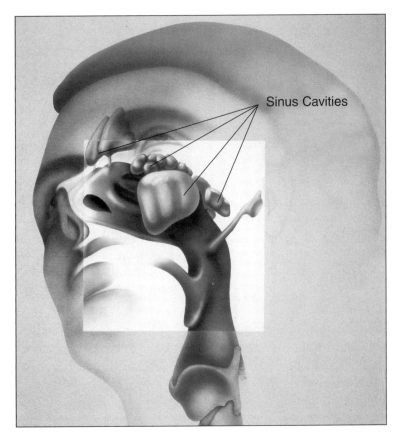

Sinus Cavities

*An illustration of the human sinus cavities.*

viruses, or fungi. These agents trigger sinusitis, which is inflammation of the sinuses. Chronic allergies can also cause swelling in the sinus cavities.

Sinusitis can be either sudden (acute) or of long duration (chronic). Both conditions produce pain and tenderness over the infected sinus. Symptoms vary, depending on which sinus cavity is inflamed. Pain may be experienced over the cheek and below the eyes, between the eyes, in the forehead, and in the back of the head. Fever, chills, red mucous membranes, fatigue, and a yellow-green nasal discharge are symptoms of sinus infection.

An acute infection of the sinuses often takes place immediately following a battle with the common cold. Swelling of the mucous membranes in the nasal cavity can block the sinus openings, causing the pressure in the sinuses to decrease. This means that the air pressure inside the sinuses is lower than atmospheric air pressure. Consequently, fluid is drawn into the sinuses, creating a site that is conducive for growth of bacteria. Once in a sinus cavity, bacteria begin to reproduce. The body responds to these invaders by sending white blood cells and fluids to the site of infection. The entry of cells and fluid increases the pressure and the pain in the sinus cavity.

Doctors can often diagnose sinusitis based on a description of the symptoms. Rest and increased fluid intake is usually advised. If symptoms are severe, antibiotics to kill the bacteria in the sinus cavities can be prescribed. Warm compresses placed on the face give some relief from discomfort. If a doctor is unsure of the diagnosis or if more information is needed about the severity of the infection, a special X-ray procedure called a CT scan may be ordered.

## Bronchitis

Chronic sinus infections can sometimes develop into a condition called bronchitis. Like the respiratory structures above them, bronchi, the tubes that extend from the trachea into the lungs, also are subject to irritation and infection. In bronchitis the mucous membranes that line the bronchi become red and swollen.

There are two forms of this disorder. Acute bronchitis comes on suddenly, often after an upper respiratory infection. It can be triggered by viruses, bacteria, or inhalation of irritating chemical or tobacco fumes. Small children and chronically ill people suffer the most from acute bronchitis. These groups are at risk of developing pneumonia as a secondary infection.

Some common symptoms of acute bronchitis are shortness of breath, chest pain, fever, chills, and coughing up sputum that contains pus. A finding of these symptoms usually gives physicians enough information to diagnose bronchitis, although chest X rays are sometimes requested as well. Before treatment, doctors attempt to determine the causative agent. When sputum is yellow or green and the patient has a high fever, bacteria are suspected and antibiotics are prescribed. When symptoms persist even after treatment with antibiotics, a lab test may be ordered. For the test, the patient is asked to cough up some sputum. The sample of sputum is then sent to the lab to grow a culture of bacteria. From the culture, the causative organism can be identified, so the correct antibiotic can be given.

Since the only therapeutic effect of antibiotics is to kill bacteria, these drugs are useless against viral infections and chemical irritants. Whatever the cause of acute bronchitis, warm vapors and decongestant sprays are recommended to open respiratory passages and reduce their swelling.

A diagnosis of chronic bronchitis is made after someone has experienced repeated attacks of acute bronchitis. In chronic bronchitis mucus production in the bronchial tubes increases. The mucosa thickens and the bronchial tubes swell, reducing the diameter of the air passage. People with this disorder feel like they cannot get enough oxygen. The thickened mucus does not drain well and sets up the possibility of further bacterial infections. Over a long period of time scars form inside the bronchi. There is no cure for chronic bronchitis, but each bacterial infection can be treated with antibiotics, and moist vapor is recommended to ease breathing.

*Chronic bronchitis causes sputum to collect in the tiny air sacs of the lungs, as shown in this illustration.*

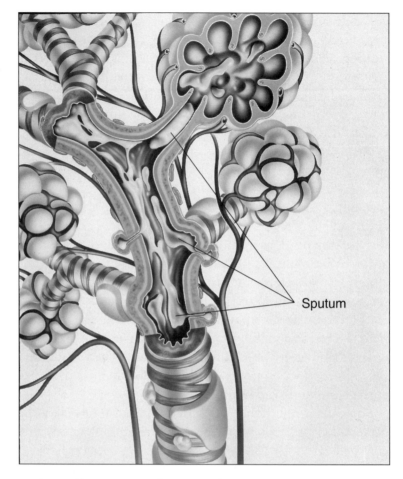

Sputum

Air pollution contributes to chronic bronchitis, but cigarette smoke is the primary cause. Statistics show that more than 50 percent of all middle-aged men who smoke twenty-five or more cigarettes a day develop chronic bronchitis. Cigarette smoke causes the lining of the bronchi to produce large amounts of mucus. The goblet cells and mucous glands of the bronchi grow in size and number, further increasing mucus production. Toxins in the cigarette smoke damage the cilia lining the bronchi. This interferes with their ability to clear the airways of excess mucus. Eventually the cilia cease to function. Mucus collects in the airway and sets up an environment where bacteria can readily multiply. Inflammation and complete destruction of cilia may result.

# Emphysema

Emphysema is another respiratory disease that can be triggered by cigarette smoke. In fact, emphysema and chronic bronchitis are collectively referred to as chronic obstructive pulmonary diseases (COPD). Smoking accounts for 85 percent of the deaths due to COPD in the United States. Research shows that some people are more genetically prone to this disorder than others. The first symptom of emphysema is usually shortness of breath. Weight loss often follows. As the disease progresses a person may eventually become unable to complete even simple daily activities.

Emphysema creates permanent changes in the lungs. Cigarette smoke causes the lung tissues to swell. Inflammation attracts white blood cells that contain enzymes capable of destroying the cell walls of the alveoli. Another enzyme in the

*Cigarette smoke damages the alveoli, and may result in the lung disease emphysema.*

body normally prevents these white blood cells from destroying the alveoli; but in people who smoke, the protective enzyme is inactivated. The alveoli in the lungs of smokers collapse and merge together to form large clusters. This reduces the surface area available for gas exchange in the lungs, so a person with emphysema does not receive enough oxygen from the alveoli. Exposure to secondhand cigarette smoke can also contribute to the development of emphysema.

The diagnosis of emphysema is similar to that of chronic bronchitis. There is no cure for emphysema, but some treatments prevent symptoms from worsening. Doctors recommend that patients not only stop smoking but also avoid secondhand smoke. Patients should also stay away from areas where the air is polluted. In severe cases of emphysema supplemental oxygen is needed along with drugs, called bronchodilators, to widen the air passages.

## Asthma

Asthma, a chronic lung disease, also causes breathing difficulty. Its symptoms are similar to those of bronchitis and emphysema. Some people who have asthma go undiagnosed because they believe they are suffering recurrent attacks of bronchitis. Shortness of breath, coughing, and tightness in the chest are some common asthma symptoms. Many asthma attacks are mild and begin with coughing or wheezing. During a severe attack the person may not be able to speak more than a few words before running out of breath. If symptoms progress to confusion, lethargy, and cyanosis, the individual is suffering from extreme oxygen deprivation. This is a medical emergency that requires immediate attention. Almost all asthma attacks, even those that are severe, can be controlled with proper treatment.

Asthma sufferers in the United States total more than 10 million people. The most disturbing statistics show that deaths due to asthma attacks increased by 35 percent between 1982 and 1992. This information has spurred scientists to learn more about what actually happens in the body during an asthma attack, and how to identify the specific agents that elicit

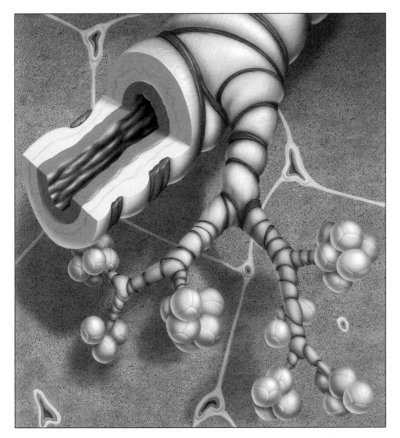

Tightened muscles (shown as dark bands) cause airways to narrow during an asthma attack.

the attack. A few of the stimuli that can trigger an episode of asthma include pollen, animal dander, dust mites, cold air, and smoke. In some people, exercise can also induce an attack.

During an asthma attack bronchi leading to the lungs swell. Mucus flows into the airways, which leads to further narrowing. The reduced diameter of the airways hinders the movement of air into and out of the lungs. Offensive stimuli in the airways probably trigger specialized cells in the bronchi to release substances such as histamine. These biochemical agents have several effects. They cause smooth muscles of the respiratory tract to swell, nasal secretions to increase, and white blood cells to flood the area. Consequently, the release of histamine can produce the characteristic shortness of breath and tightening of the chest that many asthma sufferers experience.

Doctors make their diagnosis of asthma based on medical history, physical exams, and lab tests. A lung function test can help evaluate the efficiency of the lungs. Inspection of chest X rays can reveal structural abnormalities. Blood tests measure the oxygen and carbon dioxide present in the blood. When doctors suspect that a patient's asthma is triggered by an allergen, they may recommend allergy testing. Results from the allergy tests can help identify the offending agent.

There is no cure for asthma, but there are effective ways to control or prevent symptoms. The best way to deal with asthma is to learn to identify and avoid agents that initiate attacks. If exercise is a trigger, there are medications that can be taken prior to exertion to prevent an asthma episode. Bronchodilators and corticosteroids are two medications that are often prescribed. Bronchodilators, which help to widen airways before or during an attack, also have the undesirable effect of producing rapid heart rate and restlessness. Corticosteroids are used to block inflammation and make the airways less sensitive to stimuli. Repeated use

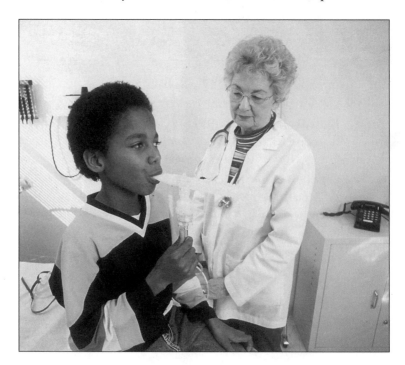

*A boy takes a lung function test to determine whether he has asthma.*

*An infant suffering from pneumonia awaits care in a hospital.*

causes adverse effects such as weight gain, swelling of the extremities, and weakening of the immune system.

## Pneumonia

Pneumonia is a disease that affects the entire lung rather than just the bronchi. It can flare up during a bout of bronchitis if bacteria or viruses slip into the lungs. In pneumonia the lungs fill with thick fluids called exudates that contain red blood cells and pus. The symptoms of this disease vary with its severity. Pneumonia sufferers may experience chest pain, fever, shortness of breath, and coughing that produces sputum. For some people nausea, vomiting, blood in the sputum, and body aches also occur.

Pneumonia usually begins after the infective organism is inhaled. However it can be carried by blood to the lungs or travel to the lungs from a nearby infection. This disorder can affect one or both of the lungs. When both lungs are involved the condition is called double pneumonia. The people most prone to developing pneumonia include very young or very old people. Also susceptible are people who are recovering from surgery, patients confined to bed, or those with poor immune function. In the United States, about 2 million people a year develop pneumonia and forty thousand to seventy thousand of these people die. Pneumonia ranks as the sixth most common cause of death in the United States. In many developing countries, pneumonia is the leading cause of death.

A physician who suspects that a patient has pneumonia will apply a stethoscope to the person's chest. This familiar device allows the user to hear chest sounds, which are abnormal when pneumonia is present. A chest X ray helps confirm diagnosis, and lab cultures of blood or sputum can identify the causative organism. If bacteria can be identified, antibiotics are given. However, viral pneumonia is not treated with this type of medication. People with very severe cases of pneumonia may be required to undergo respiratory therapy to clear secretions from their airways.

## Tuberculosis

Tuberculosis or TB is a bacterial disease that has been around since ancient times. During the Industrial Revolution tuberculosis accounted for 30 percent of all deaths in Europe. Experts believe that the high death rate was due to crowded conditions that facilitated easy transmission of the disease. Tuberculosis is a contagious disease that is transmitted by infected droplets from coughs and sneezes. When a TB victim coughs, the bacteria can remain active in the air for several hours.

Once antibiotics were developed the number of cases of tuberculosis declined. Then in the 1980s homeless shelters and prisons in the United States began to see increasing numbers of people with TB. Some cases of tuberculosis did not respond to the kind of antibiotic treatment that had been effective in the past. It was found that a number of TB bacteria have become resistant to penicillin and other drugs that have been widely used for many years. New types of antibiotics are now being employed to control the problem.

The bacterium that causes tuberculosis forms lesions, called tubercules, within the lung tissue. The first symptom is often a persistent cough accompanied by yellow-green sputum. As the disease progresses the sputum becomes streaked with blood. The patient may suffer a low-grade fever, cough, night sweats, weight loss, and feel tired all the time. Tuberculosis is not restricted to the lungs. It can travel to the kidneys, bone, lymph nodes, and joints, causing pain in these areas of the body.

TB is transmitted by inhaling air contaminated with the tuberculosis bacterium. Air contamination occurs only when a person with active TB coughs and fails to use a handkerchief to prevent the spread of bacteria-laden air. After a few days on antibiotic treatment a TB patient is no longer contagious. Most healthy people who are exposed to tuberculosis in the air never develop the disease because their immune systems are strong. However, TB bacteria can find a way into people's bodies and remain inactive or dormant in their white blood cells for years. Eventually these bacteria can result in the development of tuberculosis.

*To test for exposure to TB, a small amount of protein is injected just beneath the skin.*

This is thought to be the pattern of infection in about 80 percent of all TB cases. Dormant bacteria become active when the immune system is weakened by illness or stress, during old age, or after the use of corticosteroid drugs.

Doctors usually spot a case of tuberculosis from an abnormality that appears on a chest X-ray film. Such findings can be followed up with a test in which a small amount of protein made from the TB bacteria is injected under the skin. After a day or two, the site of the injection is checked. If redness and swelling occur, that person has been exposed to the TB bacterium at some time during his or her life. The skin test does not mean that the bacterium is active at the present time. If the test is positive, doctors often order a lab exam of sputum or fluid from the lungs to determine whether the bacteria are active.

Once uncurable, TB usually can be treated today. A combination of several antibiotics are given together to make sure that all offending bacteria are killed. However, the best way to deal with tuberculosis is through prevention. For example, some emergency room waiting areas are now equipped with a special germicidal UV or ultraviolet light that kills bacteria in the air. There are medications available for people who suspect that they have been in contact with a TB carrier.

## Pleurisy

People with lung infections like tuberculosis or pneumonia sometimes experience a pain in their chest and difficulty breathing. These symptoms may be due to pleurisy, swelling of the two pleura or membranes that cover the lungs. When these membranes are irritated they become inflamed. Fluid that accumulates between the two membranes causes uncomfortable pressure. Pleurisy can also be caused by several types of viruses and bacteria, injury, irritants, and heart failure.

People suffering from pleurisy suffer a sudden onset of chest pain. In some people the pain is sharp, but others may find it vague and difficult to pinpoint. Many experience the pain when they cough or breathe deeply. Since deep breathing hurts, people with pleurisy may use shallow, rapid breathing. In shallow breathing, chest muscles do not move very much, so pain is minimized. If fluid accumulates between the pleura, pain often disappears. However, fluid in the chest cavity puts pressure on the lungs and makes it difficult to breathe.

Pleurisy is usually diagnosed in the doctor's office after a physical examination. Listening to the patient's chest with a stethoscope, physicians can hear a distinctive rubbing sound in people with pleurisy. If the pleurisy is due to bacterial infection, antibiotics are given. All pleurisy patients may receive mild analgesics like acetaminophen or ibuprofen to relieve chest pain. A person with pleurisy is encouraged to breathe deeply and cough to expand the lungs and keep fresh air flowing through them. This helps prevent other infectious agents from colonizing lung tissue.

## Continuing Dangers from Respiratory Diseases

Although most diseases of the respiratory system share some symptoms in common, each disease is unique in its cause and treatment. In early medicine there was little treatment available for those who suffered from serious respiratory infections. It was not uncommon for people to die of influenza, pneumonia, bronchitis, tuberculosis, and asthma. Today these same illnesses are almost always treatable. Over the years doctors have developed specialized and accurate methods for diagnosing and curing respiratory illnesses.

The respiratory system is especially vulnerable to infection and chronic damage because it is exposed to the environment. Consequently, this system deals with a variety of disease-causing agents that range from viruses to chemicals. As with many other body systems, respiratory diseases are best managed by knowledge and prevention. Activities as simple as hand washing can protect against colds, flu, and a variety of other ailments. Because influenza viruses can cause severe illness, vaccines against some strains are recommended to those who get sick easily: the youngest and oldest members of society and those who have weakened immune systems.

# Medical Technology and the Respiratory System

**5**

Breathing is an essential function of the body. During breathing the respiratory system provides the body with oxygen and rids it of carbon dioxide. Health problems that make breathing difficult disrupt this essential gas exchange. That is why it is critical for the respiratory system to be in good condition.

A doctor can get some information about a patient's ailing respiratory system during an office visit. The doctor can examine the nose, mouth, and throat and listen to the patient's chest through a stethoscope to see if breathing sounds are normal. A medical history, a review of previous illnesses of the patient and the patient's family, is usually taken. This helps the doctor get an idea of the patient's genetic predispositions and previous health challenges. However, there are times when a history and physical do not provide enough information to identify and treat an illness. To gather more data laboratory tests may be needed. Scientists have developed some impressive technologies that not only help identify respiratory disorders, but also to treat them.

## Check the Blood

Following a physical examination a physician may order tests to help evaluate a breathing problem. One of the first tests performed is a blood analysis. Blood can provide information about how well the lungs are functioning. It can show how much oxygen is entering the body and how well carbon dioxide is being removed. Blood tests can be done in a doctor's office, a laboratory, or in the hospital. In a very simple procedure, a small needle inserted into an artery in the wrist removes a blood sample. This sample is then analyzed for levels of oxygen and carbon dioxide.

## Simple Tests to Evaluate Lung Function

Furthur information about lung function can be gained with a spirometric assessment. The testing equipment consists of a mouthpiece, tubing, and a recording device called a spirometer. Wearing nose clips (to prevent air escaping through the nostrils), the patient inhales and exhales air through the mouthpiece, which is attached to the drum of the spirometer by a tube. As the volume of air inside the drum changes, a piston in the spirometer moves up and down. The reading from this piston not only reveals the amount or volume of air entering and leaving the lungs, it also indicates the rate at which air flows during inhalation and exhalation.

*A man blows into a spirometer while a doctor reads the resulting graph.*

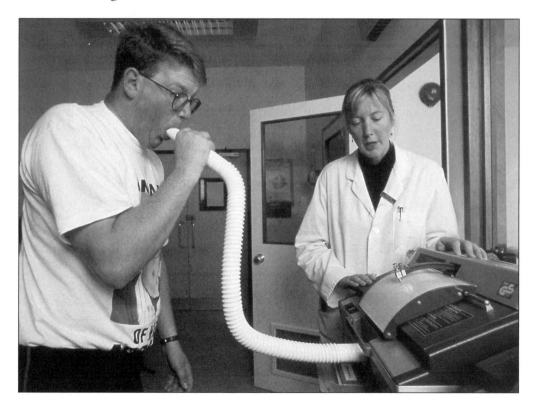

It is the elasticity of lungs, or their ability to stretch and return to normal size, that determines lung volume. Technically this property is called compliance. When lung compliance is good, lungs stretch easily and can take in a large volume of air. In some diseases, like pulmonary fibrosis, stiff scar tissue replaces normal elastic tissue in the lungs. Scar tissue is one cause of low compliance. Low compliance in diseased lungs indicates that air flow is decreased.

A spirometer can also measure the rate at which air flows into and out of the lungs. Knowing the flow rate, in turn, allows doctors to assess a patient's resistance, the extent to which movement of air is hindered. The greater the resistance, the more work a person has to expend to inhale and exhale. Resistance is high if the diameter of the airway is narrowed by swelling or the presence of mucus, as in asthma and bronchitis. More breathing problems are due to high resistance rather than to poor compliance.

## Chest X Rays

One advantage of spirometry is that the technique is noninvasive. This means that there is no penetration of the patient's body with instruments. Another noninvasive procedure is radiography, or creating pictures of the body with the invisible form of electromagnetic energy called X rays. Doctors often order a chest X ray as one of the first tests performed when patients complain of shortness of breath, persistent coughing, chest pains, or unexplained fevers. A chest X ray gives a good picture of the lungs, heart, and surrounding structures in the chest. A few conditions such as pneumonia, lung tumors, collapsed lung, fluid in the lungs, and emphysema can be clearly seen on this type of test. However, some respiratory diseases, such as chronic asthma, cannot be seen on a chest X ray. In these cases, the film may simply rule out some conditions, indicating that further testing is needed.

Chest X rays are generally performed when the patient is standing upright, unless he or she is disabled or unconscious. During the procedure an X-ray technician operates a machine that sends an X ray through the patient's chest and

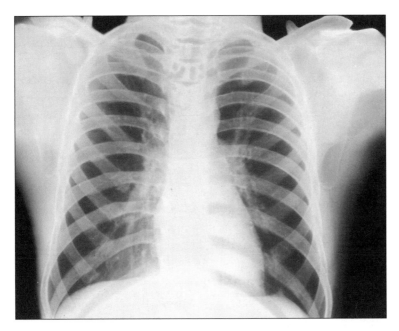

*A chest X ray shows healthy lungs (dark areas) enclosed by the ribs.*

onto a piece of radiographic film. In the fraction of the second that the X ray travels through the body, the patient must remain still and not breathe so the image does not blur. Holding the breath expands the chest and lowers the diaphragm so a good view of the lungs is produced on the film. After passing through the patient's body, the X ray exposes a photographic film. This film is placed in a machine that develops it, very much as an image is produced from film of a 35 mm camera.

Very dense objects, like the ribs, appear white or gray on film because they absorb much of the radiation. Organs which are not dense, like the lungs, appear dark on the image because they absorb little radiation. Healthy lungs have lots of air spaces, so X rays pass easily through them, and these areas appear black on the developed film. Lungs that are filled with fluid, as in the case of pneumonia, absorb radiation and appear white on the film. Tumors are dense and look like white rounded lumps on the X ray. Some cancerous tumors have small white spikes that spread out into surrounding lung tissue. Scarred lungs such as in lung fibrosis have subtle shadowing on the image.

Some X-ray equipment can digitally store the images produced on a computer. These images are saved so future X-ray films can be evaluated for changes that have occurred. The interpretation of films is the job of a radiologist, a doctor who specializes in reading X-ray images.

## Thoracentesis

If physical examination or X-ray results indicate that fluid is trapped in the cavity between the lungs and chest, a procedure called a thoracentesis or pleural tap may be used to clear the area. The lungs are protected on the outside by two pleural membranes; one covers the lungs themselves, and the other lines the chest wall. Pleural fluid between these two membranes acts as a shock absorber, and it allows the lungs to expand and contract without rubbing against chest muscles. In several conditions that cause irritation of the pleura and accumulation of pleural fluid,

*A technician examines the X ray of a patient who tested positive for TB exposure.*

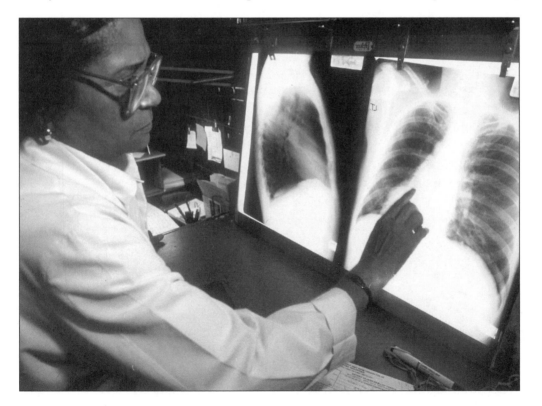

removal of some fluid has clear benefits: Analysis of pleural fluid helps determine the cause of the problem; and if a large volume of fluid has accumulated and is causing shortness of breath, its removal releases pressure and makes the patient more comfortable.

A thoracentesis can be performed in a doctor's office. The patient sits in a chair and leans forward to provide as much space as possible for the insertion of a needle between the ribs. A small area of skin on the back is cleaned and then numbed with local anesthetic. The doctor inserts a needle between the ribs into the pleural cavity and withdraws some of the fluid.

# Thoracoscopy

If a thoracentesis does not provide enough information about the condition of the pleural space and lung surface, a thoracoscopy can be performed. In this procedure a small tube called a thoracoscope is inserted into the pleural space to view the lung and membranes and to remove excess fluid in the pleural space.

In the operating room the patient is given general anesthesia. The surgeon makes three small incisions in the chest wall. Through one, the thoracoscope is inserted into the pleural space. When this happens air enters the chest cavity and the lung collapses. Through the other openings the doctor takes samples of tissue for examination under the microscope. After the procedure a tube is inserted into the pleural space to remove air that entered during the procedure. This enables the lung to reinflate.

# Bronchoscopy

If a patient's chest X-ray findings are abnormal, a test called a bronchoscopy may be performed. This is often a diagnostic procedure that simply allows the physician to view the trachea and bronchi directly, or collect samples from those areas. During a bronchoscopy a flexible tube about the diameter of a pencil is inserted into the patient's nose or mouth. Inside the tube are a bundle of cables for light transmission and auxiliary conduits for passing instruments through.

Before the testing procedure, the patient's throat and nasal passages are anesthetized to prevent coughing and gagging; in some cases the patient also is given general anesthesia to induce deep sleep. After insertion the bronchoscope slowly travels through the respiratory tract. If the physician sees an abnormal region, tissue samples can be collected, either by means of biopsy forceps threaded through the bronchoscope or by suctioning off cells loosened by saline washing. In both cases the samples retrieved are later evaluated under the microscope.

The bronchoscope can also be used to treat problems in the airways. Through its channels a host of procedures can be performed: foreign bodies removed, laser therapy delivered, and lung abscesses drained. Video chip bronchoscopes also record images for further evaluation. After the procedure is completed the patient cannot eat or drink for a couple of hours because their swallowing and cough reflexes have been depressed.

## Bronchography

To preserve the findings of a bronchoscopy, an X ray called a bronchogram can be taken. This is an X-ray image of the trachea and bronchial tree. It is often used to help locate obstructions, cysts, or tumors. In bronchography, a material that absorbs X rays and shows up well on film is sent down the bronchoscope. This so-called contrast medium coats the airways, enabling their outlines to be seen on X-ray film. Once the contrast material is in place, the position of the patient is adjusted in various ways to force the contrast material to move into all parts of the bronchi. At the same time X rays are made which help reveal any abnormal structures that are present.

## CT Scans: The Body in 3-D

The development of scanning cameras equipped for computerized tomography (CT) offers a different inside view of the respiratory system. Unlike two-dimensional chest X rays or bronchograms, CT scans create three-dimensional cross-sectional images of the inside of the body. For example, a thoracic CT scan passes X rays through the thorax at dif-

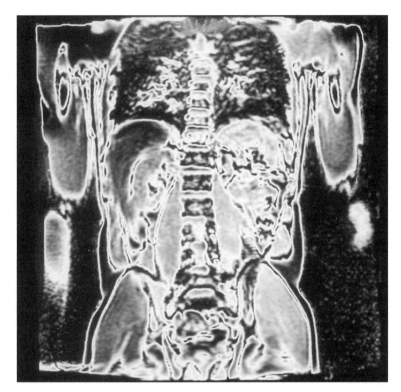

*A CT scan reveals a three-dimensional view of a human thorax from the inside out.*

ferent angles; each image is recorded by the scanner's computer, resulting in three-dimensional pictures that are very useful in seeing small differences in tissue density. The CT scan provides so much detail that small lesions of tuberculosis can be distinguished from benign or malignant tumors in the lungs.

Prior to the scan patients are sometimes injected with a contrast agent to improve visual discrimination. During the CT scan the patient reclines on a table that is positioned in the center of a ring-shaped piece of X-ray equipment called the scanner. As the patient lies still the scanner rotates 360 degrees around the part of the patient being examined. As it moves from the top to the sides, then underneath the patient, the scanner emits rays and immediately picks up their reflections. The reflected rays are fed into a computer which analyzes the information and calculates the differences in density of various tissues, water, fat, bone, and air. The computer uses this information to construct a picture on a screen.

As in two-dimensional X rays, black and white areas are air and bone, respectively, while shades of gray show water, fat, and soft tissues which cannot be distinguished on two-dimensional film. CT scans can reveal abnormal conditions such as tumors, nodules, and accumulations of blood, fluid, and fat in the lungs.

## Nuclear Medicine

Another type of imaging uses nuclear or radioactive isotopes. Radioisotopes are atomic particles that emit radiation. This imaging method is similar to a CT scan, but a small amount of radioactive material is added to the contrast medium to promote visualization of internal tissues that cannot otherwise be seen. When radioactive contrast medium is given to a patient, it is absorbed by some tissues but not others. These tissues can be viewed with the help of a device called a gamma camera. It detects the amount and location of the radiation (gamma rays) given off by the radioactive substance. This information is sent to a computer, which assimilates it and creates an image.

In another nuclear test, the lung perfusion scan, the flow of blood through the lungs is imaged. This scan is done to see if there is blockage of the blood vessels in the lungs. A solution containing radioisotopes is injected into the patient's bloodstream. The gamma camera detects the route the radioactive material takes as it travels through the lungs. Absence of radioactive material in an area tells the doctor that no blood is flowing through the area because some of the lung is damaged. This indicates either lung disease or blockage of the pulmonary artery leading to the lungs from the heart. Images from the gamma camera appear as so-called hot and cold spots. Hot spots are places where radioisotopes are taken up, and they indicate normal lung function. Cold spots are areas where radioactive material is not found, and they suggest an abnormality. To confirm an abnormal finding, another type of nuclear scan, a lung ventilation test, is done.

The lung ventilation scan involves the use of air mixed with radioactive gas such as xenon or krypton. The patient inhales the radioactive gas, which spreads through the lungs. A gamma camera monitors the distribution of the gas in the lungs. Ideally, the distribution of gases will be equal in both lungs. Low radioactivity in an area means that an airway may be obstructed.

The results of lung perfusion and lung ventilation scans are used together to make a diagnosis. If a pulmonary artery is blocked, perfusion test results are poor, but ventilation tests are normal. If pneumonia is present in the lung, the ventilation test is abnormal. The use of the two tests together can help doctors distinguish between diseases such as emphysema, cancer, and tuberculosis.

## Artificial Ventilators

A person who is unable to breathe, perhaps because of emphysema, pneumonia, or severe asthma, is in respiratory distress. Artificial respiration may be needed temporarily to keep that person alive. During artificial respiration air is forced into and out of the lungs. If a person is not breathing,

*Unable to breathe on his own, this patient requires an artificial respirator while he recovers from heart surgery.*

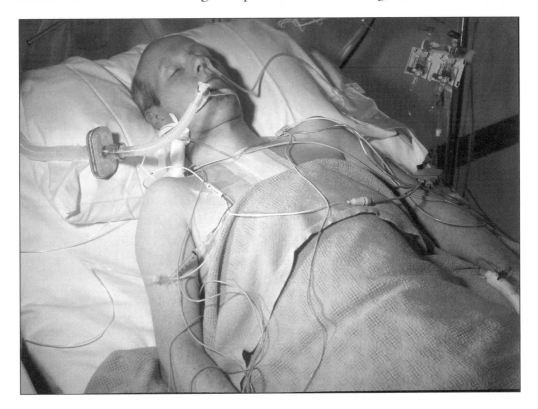

artificial respiration should be started immediately. The mouth-to-mouth method can be used until help arrives. Emergency room technicians and paramedics carry a portable resuscitator for such situations.

If the patient is still unable to breathe without assistance after an hour or more, doctors may need a device called an artificial ventilator. Artificial ventilators are used when the respiratory muscles cannot do the work required to expand the chest cavity. The respirator supports breathing until the patient is able to resume the process without assistance. The machines are lifesavers when the lungs have been damaged in an accident or as a result of a chronic disease. They are also helpful in disease processes like pulmonary fibrosis in which lungs become so stiff they cannot expand. Stiff lungs fill with fluid and interfere with normal function.

To help the patient breathe, the doctor inserts a tube through the nose, mouth, or an incision in the trachea. The free end of the tube is connected to the computerized pump of the ventilation machine. The pump generates the energy necessary for gases to be moved into and out of the lungs. The energy from the machine takes over the job of inflating and deflating the lungs that is usually done by respiratory muscles of the patient. Before air passes from the ventilator into the lungs it is first fed through a humidifier that is part of the machine. This moistens air and prevents the lungs from becoming too dry. Computerized controls on the ventilator regulate the duration of each breath, the pressure applied to the airway, and the oxygen concentration. Medical personnel also monitor a patient's heart rate and blood pressure to make sure the ventilator is functioning at the best rate for that person's condition.

There are two types of artificial ventilators in use today: conventional and high frequency ventilators. The most common one is the conventional ventilator found in intensive care units, operating rooms, and ambulances. Patients of all ages can use this type of ventilator. It simulates a normal breathing pattern for a person at rest. This is usually twelve to twenty-five breaths per minute for an adult or

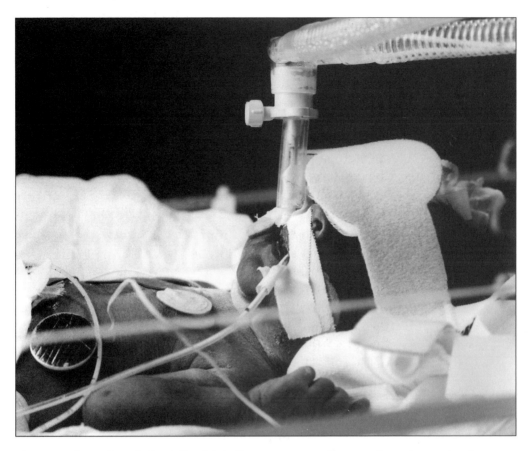

thirty to forty for a baby. The high frequency ventilator, often used with newborn infants and very old patients, creates frequent shallow breaths that do not fully expand the lungs. This type of breathing reduces stress on lungs that are not able to stretch to full capacity. It protects fragile lung tissue like that seen in premature babies.

*The artificial ventilator attached to this baby will deliver short, shallow breaths to protect its underdeveloped lungs.*

## Bringing It All Together

Every cell in the human body must have oxygen to survive. The acquisition and delivery of that oxygen is the job of the respiratory system. For the most part, the human respiratory system works on autopilot. Without ever giving it a thought, people breathe in and out about twenty times a minute. During exercise breathing rate goes up; in sleep it slows down. Breathing is so reliable and constant that most people take it for granted.

However, breathing becomes noticeable when it is difficult. When there is little or no air available, the job of delivering oxygen to cells is a challenge. Those who engage in sports under extreme conditions often need special training to accommodate the needs of their respiratory systems. Explorers to mountain peaks and ocean valleys have learned to take advantage of the natural abilities of their lungs to cope and adapt. The thin air found at high elevations puts a strain on the lungs of any novice mountain climber. Yet with a little time, the respiratory system of even a lowlander can adapt remarkably well to its new challenges. Likewise, those who explore the ocean's depths must have special knowledge of lung function and gas absorption to survive.

Most people who experience difficulty in breathing, however, are not adventurers. More breathing problems result from illness than from any other cause. Lungs can be temporarily or permanently damaged by disease. Many diseases interfere with the lungs' ability to mechanically bring in air. Others damage the lungs on the gas exchange level and prevent oxygen from entering the blood.

At one time there was little medical practitioners could do for their patients who had trouble breathing. One of the earliest medical instruments for examining the respiratory system was a crude bronchoscope. To see the larynx and trachea a physician inserted a viewing instrument made of a rod, a candle, and a crude mirror into the patient's mouth. Thanks to modern medicine and its technologies it is much easier and safer now for doctors to diagnose and treat respiratory problems.

# GLOSSARY

**apnea:** Cessation of breathing.

**capillary:** Extremely small blood vessel.

**cell membrane:** Plasma membrane that separates a cell from its environment.

**chronic:** Of long duration.

**cohesion:** The attraction of like particles to each other.

**cyanosis:** Blue coloration of skin due to reduction of oxygen in blood.

**decongestant:** Medication that clears blocked nasal passages and sinuses.

**diagnosis:** Identification of disease or disorder by examination and analysis.

**diffuse:** To passively move from an area of high concentration to an area of low concentration.

**emphysema:** A disease characterized by ruptured alveoli; symptoms include impaired airflow, breathing difficulty, and cough.

**expire:** To push air from lungs.

**inflammation:** Localized heat, redness, and swelling.

**inspire:** To draw air into lungs.

**metabolism:** Sum total of all chemical reactions within an organism, including multiple metabolic pathways to process different substances, such as oxygen.

**nasal mucosa:** Mucous membrane of the nose that contains mucus-secreting cells.

**phlegm:** Stringy, thick mucus produced by the respiratory tract.

**pulmonary:** Relating to the lungs.

**pulmonary fibrosis:** Formation of fibrous or scarlike tissue in the lungs.

**secondhand smoke:** Cigarette smoke inhaled by persons other than smokers.

**strain:** Group of organisms of the same species that have distinctive characteristics.

**ventilator:** A machine that takes over breathing function, inflating and deflating lungs; also called a respirator.

**X ray:** An invisible form of electromagnetic radiation that can penetrate tissues.

# FOR FURTHER READING

## Books

Elizabeth Fong, *Body Structures and Functions*. St. Louis, MO: Times Mirror/Mosby Publishers, 1987. Provides simple and thorough description of various diseases of the human body.

Alma Guinness, *ABC's of the Human Body*. Pleasantville, NY: Reader's Digest, 1987. Discusses the various structures of the human body and addresses some interesting reasons for certain body functions.

*The Handy Science Answer Book*. Canton, MI: The Visible Ink Press, 1997. Gives very cute explanations for a variety of happenings in the science world.

*How in the World?* Pleasantville, NY: Reader's Digest, 1990. This book provides an interesting coverage of both physical and biological events that occur in life.

David E. Larson, *Mayo Clinic Family Health Book*. New York: William Morrow, 1996. Describes in simple terms the many diseases that can affect the human body.

Susan McKeever, *The Dorling Kindersley Science Encyclopedia*. New York: Dorling Kindersley, 1994. Gives concise information on physical and biological occurrences in life. Good illustrations help to explain topics.

Mary Lou Mulvihill, *Human Diseases*. Norwalk, CT: Appleton & Lange, 1995. Provides a good description of the most common diseases of the human body.

*World Book Medical Encyclopedia*. Chicago: World Book, 1995. Provides a vast amount of information on the physiology of the human body systems.

## Internet Sources

Electronic Library Encyclopedia, "Decompression Sickness," 2001. www.encyclopedia.com.

How Stuff Works, "How the Lungs Work," 1998. www.howstuff works.com.

How Stuff Works, "Scuba Diving and the Bends," 1998. www.howstuff works.com.

MSNBC Health Newsletter, "Why Do We Yawn?" 2001. www.msnbc.com.

*Science News World,* "Breathing on the Edge," March 31, 2001. www.science news.org.

Think Quest Library, "Diving: Human Contact with the Underwater World," 2001. www.thinkquest.org.

## Websites

**Diving to Great Depths** (www.seagrant.com). Researcher Claes Lundgren discusses how the human body copes with extreme conditions of underwater diving.

**Mehgan Heaney-Frier Free Diver** (www.freediver.com). Free diver Mehgan Heaney-Frier tells how she can stay underwater for four-and-one-half minutes, a record-setting breath hold dive.

# WORKS CONSULTED

## Books

Robert Berkow, *The Merck Manual of Medical Information*. New York: Pocket Books, 1997. Provides a detailed explanation of all human respiratory organs. This book gives information on the causes, symptoms, diagnosis, and treatment of many respiratory diseases.

Charles B. Clayman, *The Respiratory System*. Pleasantville, NY: Reader's Digest, 1992. Provides information on the structures, functions, and possible abnormalities of the respiratory organs.

Charlotte Dienhart, *Basic Human Anatomy and Physiology*. Philadelphia: W.B. Saunders, 1979. This textbook covers the structure and function of all organ systems in the human body. It also provides information on symptoms and treatments of various diseases.

William C. Goldberg, *Clinical Physiology Made Ridiculously Simple*. Miami, FL: Med Masters, 1995. This booklet gives a very detailed explanation of the function of all organs in the respiratory system. Illustrations reinforce the written content.

John Hole Jr., *Essentials of Human Anatomy and Physiology*. Dubuque, IA: Wm. C. Brown, 1992. This textbook of anatomy and physiology provides detailed explanations of the structure and function of all human respiratory organs.

Anthony L. Komaroff, *Harvard Medical School Family Health Guide*. New York: Simon and Schuster, 1999. This book provides comprehensive coverage of the various disorders and diseases that can affect the human body. Symptoms, causes, diagnosis, and treatment options are provided.

Ann Kramer, *The Human Body, The World Book Encyclopedia of Science*. Chicago: World Book, 1987. Provides information on all body systems as well as explanations about unusual and interesting events that occur in the human body.

Stanley Loeb, *The Illustrated Guide to Diagnostic Tests*. Springhouse, PA: Springhouse, 1994. This medical book gives a very thorough description and explanation of how and why medical technologies are employed to diagnose and treat human diseases and disorders.

Elaine Marieb, *Human Anatomy and Physiology*. Redwood City, CA: Benjamin/Cummings, 1995. Offers a very detailed explanation of all human body structures and organs.

## Websites

**Cornell Medical College** (www. edcenter.med.cornell.edu). The medical college of Cornell provides a wide range of information on body systems. Select respiratory system in search. A detailed lecture on the structure and function of the respiratory system is provided with special emphasis on gas exchange.

**Davidson College Biology Department** (www.bio.davidson.edu). In the search field, type in "research on the physiological effects of high altitudes" to get several advanced scientific studies.

**The Merck Manual** (www.merck.com). This website gives a detailed explanation of respiratory diseases as well as information on the stresses of altitude sickness on the human respiratory tract.

**NOLS Wilderness First Aid** (www. nols.edu). By selecting Altitude Illness on this site, a detailed description of mountain illnesses, respiratory adaptations, and acclimatization is provided.

# INDEX

# PICTURE CREDITS

# ABOUT THE AUTHORS

Both Pam Walker and Elaine Wood have degrees in biology and education from colleges in Georgia. They have taught science in grades seven through twelve since the mid–1980s.

Ms. Walker and Ms. Wood are coauthors of more than a dozen science teacher resource activity books and two science textbooks.